Platonic Mysticism

Series in Western Esoteric Traditions

David Appelbaum, editor

Platonic Mysticism

Contemplative Science, Philosophy, Literature, and Art

ARTHUR VERSLUIS

Cover image: Thomas Cole, *View from Mount Holyoke, Northampton, Massachusetts, after a Thunderstorm—The Oxbow.* 1836. Oil on canvas.

Published by State University of New York Press, Albany

For information, contact State University of New York Press, Albany, NY
www.sunypress.edu

Production, Eileen Nizer
Marketing, Fran Keneston

Library of Congress Cataloging-in-Publication Data

Names: Versluis, Arthur, 1959– author.
Title: Platonic mysticism : contemplative science, philosophy, literature, and art / by Arthur Versluis.
Description: Albany, NY : State University of New York, 2017. | Series: SUNY series in western esoteric traditions | Includes bibliographical references and index.
Identifiers: LCCN 2016044213 (print) | LCCN 2017033130 (ebook) | ISBN 9781438466347 (ebook) | ISBN 9781438466330 (hardcover : alk. paper) | ISBN 9781438466323 (pbk. : alk. paper)
Subjects: LCSH: Plato. | Mysticism.
Classification: LCC B398.M77 (ebook) | LCC B398.M77 V47 2017 (print) | DDC 204/.22—dc23
LC record available at https://lccn.loc.gov/2016044213

10 9 8 7 6 5 4 3 2 1

Contents

Acknowledgments

Platonic Mysticism, a sequel to *Restoring Paradise: Western Esotericism, Literature, Art, and Consciousness* (SUNY Press, 2004), is dedicated to the memory of my father, who would have very much enjoyed reading it in its final form. I am grateful to colleagues with whom I have shared parts of the book, for their suggestions and ideas. I'd like to thank the colleagues associated with Hieros [www.hieros.world], as well as Dr. David R. Fideler for his perceptive observations, and Dr. John Richards, who forecast that esoteric studies would become part of consciousness studies. That in turn made this book possible. Part of chapter 4, "The Externalist Fallacy," appears in *Esoterica*, www.esoteric.msu.edu. The article's copyright belongs to the author, but our thanks to Michigan State University for hosting the journal.

Introduction

This book is intended to fill a signal absence in the literature on mysticism. Scanning the titles published on the subject of mysticism over the past several decades, and those scheduled as forthcoming titles, one is startled by how few there are, and how tangential, in many cases, their relationship often is to the way the term "mysticism" was historically understood in the academic world. What a tangle one finds when reading over the literature on mysticism of the past century, and especially of the past several decades! Mysticism, it sometimes seems, could be almost anything, in any religion, at any time. By contrast, the purpose of this book is to refocus the discussion on mysticism and to restore an important context for understanding the term. That context, taken for granted a century ago, must be reconsidered in a new light. The argument in this book is that "mysticism" as a descriptor becomes intellectually incoherent if we don't recognize and acknowledge its Platonic history and context.

Of course, there are few religious terms more anathematized than "mysticism." It is not uncommon to find the word used for denigration, as when an economic analyst is condemned because his predictive work is based on nothing more than "mysticism," or when an analytical philosopher makes the word synonymous with confusion and wooly-mindedness. Typically these dismissals include a phrase like "nothing more than," because after all, mysticism is, as it were, the very bottom of the barrel. In contemporary scholarship on religion, one finds relatively little being published on the topic, and one might wonder why that is.

The current drift of contemporary scholarship is well away from an unfashionable subject like mysticism. Scholars are no less subject to the biases or inclinations of the age, after all. Hence one finds considerable emphasis on the study of "material culture," which by its nature tends to discourage questions of meaning, purpose, cosmology or metaphysics. Instead, one can stay safely ensconced in areas that allow one to creep over the surface of things. "Essentialism" is an epithet often used to set aside questions of higher meaning.[1] Many seem to have bought into a prevailing assertion that "nothing is true," even if for some reason or another everything is not permitted, or alternatively, that there is no truth in any absolute sense. Behind such perspectives is typically a shallow materialism, as visible in Marxism as it is in other forms of reductionism. In brief, we live in an era of extreme relativism, and one in which subjects like mysticism or transcendence are not in vogue, to say the least.

One hundred years ago that was not the case: then, mysticism was broadly understood to represent the center and apex of religious experience. Authors such as William James and Evelyn Underhill viewed mysticism as the touchstone for understanding religious experience because it represented direct inner realization of transcendent reality or the Divine. Authors prior to and after James and Underhill in the early twentieth century—often based on very wide and deep reading in the classic mystical texts from late antiquity to that time—saw mysticism as the immediate spiritual intuition of truth or truths believed to transcend reason, or as a deep linking (sometimes, uniting) of the soul with God through contemplative or ecstatic illumination.[2]

Of course typical definitions of mysticism often include a secondary definition as varied as "wooly-minded speculation" or "obscure thought" or "belief not based on evidence" or "belief not subjected to criticism," as well as "subjective experiences" that include "séances" and "astral projection [!]." And indeed, not every experience alleged to be mystical is necessarily so, but these kinds of secondary definitions go beyond that point to, in essence, dismiss the very notion of mysticism as worthy of one's attention. Bundling mysticism up with spiritualism (channeling what are held to be the spirits of the dead), séances, or astral projection only confuses the matter further.

It may be best, in the end, simply to jettison the word "mysticism" in favor of a term perhaps more precise, like B. Alan Wallace's preference, "contemplative science."[3] Certainly terms like "contemplative science," "mindfulness," or "contemplative practice" carry less baggage than the word "mysticism." I confess that I have thought quite seriously about giving this book a different title and a different terminology, perhaps one drawn from Neoplatonism.[4] But "contemplative practice" or "contemplative studies," by engaging the word "contemplation," implies all that goes under that term, and so dilutes the subject under consideration. There are advantages to terms derived from "contemplative," but also disadvantages, the chief of which is that whereas "mysticism" emphasizes direct inner spiritual knowledge of the transcendence of subject and object, "contemplation" is more diffuse, and emphasizes process over result.

"Mysticism," like it or not, has a long history; it's the accepted term; and confusion about what it means doesn't invalidate it, but rather calls for a more precise definition. Etymology often helps clarify meaning. The word "mysticism" derives from the Greek *mystikos* (μυστικός), meaning secret or esoteric path of the mysteries, and derives from *mystes* (μύστης), meaning an initiate into the mysteries, or more literally, one who has seen directly for himself or herself into the mysteries. Given its accumulated meanings over millennia, "mysticism" can be understood to refer more broadly to religious experiences corresponding to the direct cognition of a transcendent reality beyond the division of subject and object.

Defining mysticism as "direct cognition of a transcendent reality beyond the division of subject and object" has numerous advantages. First, it makes clear that mysticism is a type of cognition. Second, it recognizes that this kind of cognition is beyond instrumentalizing rationality that infers what is true; it is, rather, direct cognition of a "transcendent reality," without thereby limiting what that term means except to say that it is "beyond the division of subject and object." Hence, third, while precise, this definition is also broad enough to include both apophatic and visionary mysticism. The transcendence of subject and object can be understood as taking place on a continuum. The heart of this transcendence is known as *via negativa*, or apophatic experience, meaning the fundamental or primordial reality beyond any conceptual and sensory representation. But the same definition also holds for visionary experiences that take place hierophanically, in an inner dimension where the observing subject is not separate from the revealing object, but rather where the divine "other" reveals itself to "me."

This terminology derives from the source for mysticism, Dionysius the Areopagite, who probably lived in the fifth century AD. Dionysius represents the confluence of Platonism with Christianity, and some have speculated that Dionysius was in fact a famous Platonist who translated Platonism into a Christian context when it became clear that pagan Platonism was not long to survive. Such a hypothesis may well be true. But whether it is so or not, Christian mysticism throughout its subsequent history can be fully understood only with reference to the seminal figure of Dionysius the Areopagite. It is scarcely an exaggeration to say that Dionysius, in his terse treatises, created a framework for all of Western mysticism. In this book, I argue that mysticism is best understood not just as a nebulous catch-all term applicable for all kinds of phenomena in many or all religions, but rather first of all as it was understood for much of history—as Christian mysticism in the tradition of Dionysius the Areopagite. This tradition is best termed "Platonic mysticism." And here we will briefly sketch what that means.

Essential to understanding this frame are the concepts of *via positiva* and *via negativa*. Dionysius discusses the *via positiva*, or way of images, in his *Celestial Hierarchy*. He writes, "It is therefore lawful to portray Celestial Beings in forms drawn from even the lowest of material things [because they too have] some vestiges of Intellectual Beauty, and through these we may be led to immaterial Archetypes."[5] Through sacred symbols and images we can ascend in contemplation to the divine archetypes, and this ascent through images is sometimes termed "kataphatic mysticism." The word "kataphatic" derives from the Greek *kata-* [to descend, or downward movement] and *phanai*, meaning to speak or to reveal. Effectively, the kataphatic or *via positiva* forms of mysticism are *affirmative* in the sense that they offer an ascent through images, symbols, and words/conceptual analogies that "descend" from "above."

The danger, of course, is that the rational mind reifies an analogical likeness and "fixes" it conceptually, turning it into a dogmatic assertion that in fact blocks one's understanding. For this reason, Dionysius remarks that unlike symbols are often better than analogies, because by their very nature, an unlike or even dissonant symbol resists or deflects conceptual reification or fixation. Focusing on a particular symbol or image can be a path through the image to transcendence, but it also can produce a conceptual construct that paradoxically serves to block the transcendence that is, after all, the point of both the *via affirmativa* and the *via negativa*, since both are paths or approaches to direct knowledge (gnosis).

But whereas the *via positiva* is ascent through images and symbols, the *via negativa* or apophatic way is ascent through the negation of all conceptual analogues. Whereas the cataphatic approach is affirmative, the apophatic (from the Greek *apo-*, or "no" and *phanai*, "saying," literally, "saying no") is the way of negation. By systematically denying what the experience of the transcendent is like, one not only removes misunderstanding, but also clears space for one's own direct perception. Dionysius writes in the seminal treatise *Mystical Theology* that "the higher we soar in contemplation, the more limited become our expressions of that which is purely intelligible." Hence, when "plunging into the Darkness that is above the intellect, we pass not merely into brevity of speech, but even into absolute silence of thoughts and of words."[6] For the divine transcendence is not soul, nor intellect, nor sensory perception; it is not essence, or eternity, or time; it cannot be attained or grasped by reason; it cannot even be affirmed or denied, for it belongs to an entirely different order than what can be conceived or understood through conceptualization; it transcends affirmation and negation and is free from any limitation whatsoever.[7]

Both the affirmative and the negative ways derive from and exist in a larger philosophico-religious context: Platonism. In order to clearly delineate and understand what mysticism is, one first has to understand its Platonic origin. As I discussed in detail in *Perennial Philosophy*, Platonism is best understood as a conceptual map for understanding contemplative ascent and illumination. Here I am referring to Platonism in its entirety as a tradition, beginning of course with Plato, but also including the so-called "middle" and "late" Platonists, from Plotinus to Damascius, the last head of the Platonic Academy. Platonism in this context means the whole of the tradition, and it also means the distillation of that tradition into the individual ascent from the Cave of ignorance to the Light of transcendent, unitive knowledge.

In essence, of course, Plato himself conveyed essential aspects of the secret initiatory traditions inherited from Egypt by Greece, but he conveyed them in literary, metaphorical, and hence individualized form. Whereas the Mystery traditions were community experiences, Plato conveyed some aspects of them in philosophico-literary language in order to make them accessible to the individual reader. Hence in *Phaedrus*, Plato describes the individual ascent as if one were to grow wings; and in his *Symposium*, he conveys aspects of the Mysteries of eros in literary form through the character Diotima, the female initiate. What we see expressed in the seminal dialogues of *Phaedrus, Symposium, Republic,* and even *Timaeus* and the letters is not philosophy in the restricted modern sense of combatively expressed discursive rationalist analysis, but rather is philosophico-religious, that is, philosophy introduces us to an overview of contemplative ascent and illumination that is independent of any confessional religious context.

We see this nonconfessional, practical tradition most clearly, not so much in Plato's dialogues—because Plato is allusive, coy, and enigmatic—but rather in Plotinus's *Enneads.* For understanding mysticism, Plotinus is essential. The *Enneads* are comprised of six groups of nine treatises, hence the name (from Greek *ennea,* nine). These six books were arranged by Plotinus's follower Porphyry, who organized them thematically from individual ethical concerns through cosmology, the nature of the soul, knowledge and individual transcendence, and the nature of the transcendent One. For our purposes, although there are gems scattered throughout the *Enneads,* the most important books are the fifth and sixth, in which Plotinus narrates aspects of the path from subject-object dualism to transcendent knowledge of ultimate reality.

Much of the fifth book is devoted to details of the ascent from duality to unity, and to whether and to what extent the intelligible or archetypal realm participates in what he terms "the One." Plotinus tells us that "the ascent must be made to a one, and this means truly one, but not one like all other things which are multiple and one by participation in a one," for rather, the One must be grasped in itself, so in this course the contemplative must not move in the least bit towards duality.[8] Beyond all duality is the First, and from this transcendence depends the Intellect.[9] Even the name "the One" is merely provisional, Plotinus tells us, and "perhaps this name [the One] was given it in order that the seeker, beginning from this which is completely indicative of simplicity, may finally negate this as well."[10]

Intellect, veiling itself from the phenomenal world and "drawing itself inward," without looking at anything in particular, will "see a light," and this light is neither within nor without. And indeed, Plotinus continues, "one should not enquire whence it comes, for there is no 'whence,' since it does not really come or go away anywhere."[11] "So," Plotinus advises, "one must not chase after it, but wait quietly till it appears, preparing oneself to contemplate it, as the eye awaits the rising of the sun."[12] And what is the horizon above which the sun will mount? It is Intellect. For Intellect turns and gives itself in contemplation to the Beautiful, which does not come as expected, but "as one who did not come," "for he was seen, not as having come, but as being there before all things, even before Intellect came. It is Intellect which comes, and again Intellect which goes away, because it does not know where to stay and where he stays, that is in nothing." Were it possible for Intellect to abide in that nowhere, it would be one with him, not two. It is a wonder, Plotinus tells us, "how he is present without having come, and how, though he is nowhere, there is nowhere he is not."[13]

What we see here clearly in Plotinus's *Enneads* is the way of negation carefully described in experiential terms. This way of negation is central to understanding Plotinus's metaphysics, but it is also central to understanding *how* Plotinus arrives at and experiences the stages of transcendence that his metaphysics describes. Plotinus's treatises, and particularly the fifth and sixth books of his *Enneads*, as we can see in the passages quoted above, are clearly experiential in origin—he seeks to convey, in metaphorical language, what he has experienced and even to some extent at least, how he came to that experience of transcendence. At the heart of that transcendence is the paradox that Intellect is experiencing "nothing," "nowhere," a transcendence that is present everywhere even though it never arrives anywhere because it is always there, and even though it is there, that "there" is "nowhere."

In the sixth book, Plotinus confides some secrets of what we may call a spiritual anthropology in the form of a kind of spiritual reminiscence. He observes that in the "primeval" transcendent realm, there is no division, even though it may seem that there is. And we as individuals who exist in time, before coming to be "we were there," "some of us even gods, pure souls and intellect united with the whole of reality; we were parts of the intelligible," and indeed "we are not cut off even now."[14] This primeval transcendent reality is our true home; it is the ground of all that is; and it is possible for us to recognize it anew, because it does not ever change; it does not belong to the realm of transience, even though it is present throughout it.

I have dwelled here on Plotinus's *Enneads* because his extraordinary work offers us both a metaphysical context and experiential hints concerning the nature of mysticism. Mysticism, in the context we are exploring in this book, is the contemplative ascent of the individual from duality to subject-object transcendence, and as such even though we each experience such an ascent through our own particular path, nonetheless as Plotinus puts it, "I do not touch one Good, and you another, but the same, and not the same in such a way that one stream comes from it to me and another to you."[15] Rather, the transcendent is one, unitary, existing outside all time, abiding in eternity, unbounded, immeasurable.[16] Mysticism is a word for coming to recognize transcendent reality for oneself.

We begin this new look at mysticism with Plato, Plotinus, and Dionysius the Areopagite because this context provides us with a much clearer framework for understanding what mysticism is. And when we understand the term and the concept within the larger context of Platonism, we also begin to understand much more clearly the historical exemplars of mysticism. Mysticism can be understood just as Evelyn Underhill put it, as "the nature and development of man's spiritual consciousness."[17] Mysticism is the awakening of reflective awareness of our own transcendent nature, or to put it another way, of the nature of transcendent reality from which, in this tradition, it is said we are indivisible. As such, mysticism has offshoots and subsets that can better be understood with reference to it, but mysticism essentially is contemplative ascent and illumination, whatever cultural context it exists within. The same, of course, may be said of Platonism itself; for our purposes, Platonism and mysticism are different terms for the same thing. Succinctly put, the best way to express our primary subject in this book is "Platonic mysticism."

CHAPTER ONE

Platonic Mysticism

In the introduction, we began with the etymology of the word "mysticism," which derives from *mystes* (μύστης), an initiate into the ancient Mysteries. Literally, it refers to "one who remains silent," or to "that which is concealed," referring one's direct inner experience of transcendence that cannot be fully expressed discursively, only alluded to. Of course, it is not clear what the Mysteries revealed; the Mystery revelations, as Walter Burkert suggested, may have been to a significant degree cosmological and magical.[1] But it is clear that there is a related Platonic tradition that, while it begins with Plato's dialogues, is most clearly expressed in Plotinus and is conveyed in condensed form into Christianity by Dionysius the Areopagite. Here, we will introduce the Platonic nature of mysticism.

That we focus on this current of mysticism originating with Plato and Platonism and feeding into Christianity should not be understood as suggesting that there is no mysticism in other traditions. Rather, by focusing on Christian mysticism, we will see much more clearly what is meant by the term "mysticism," and *because* we are concentrating on a particular tradition, we will be able to recognize whether and to what extent similar currents are to be found in other religious traditions. At the same time, to understand Christian mysticism, we must begin with Platonism, because the Platonic tradition provides the metaphysical context for understanding its latest expression in Christian mysticism.

Plato himself is, of course, a sophisticated author of fiction who puts nearly all of what he wrote into the form of literary dialogues between various characters. Hardly anything he wrote can be attributed fully to him, because what constitutes Plato's thought really belongs to his characters—making Platonism uniquely oblique as philosophico-religious expression. But such a literary approach allowed Plato to express in coyly allusive ways what I have elsewhere termed "the contemplative ascent" and "illumination." This approach also meant that Platonism was not bound to ancient paganism but could be introduced comfortably into other religious traditions, including Christianity. The metaphysics is portable.

Plato expresses himself in figures, analogies, symbols: mysticism in Plato is expressed indirectly, in terms of wingéd ascent, as remembrance of truth, as initiation into mysteries, but not, for the most part, in terms of pure transcendence. In *Phaedrus*, Plato famously describes as a kind of erotic madness the desire of the soul to ascend to authentic and true beauty when seeing beauty on earth, or the beauty of the beloved. What we long for, in this kind of madness, is the "most blessed" "beatific vision" of our initiation into the mystery of the realm of the gods, "shining in pure light." We remember this primordial vision, Plato tells us, and we long to return to it.[2] He describes how the lover, upon seeing the beloved, begins to grow wings and to undergo both pain and joy as he seeks to ascend. Because of our desire for the beloved, we are willing to give up all other earthly things, happily living in poverty if only we can be near our beloved, and through our love we enter into a "happy band" of those who live in the realm of light.[3]

A very similar vision is outlined in *Symposium*, where the stranger woman Diotima of Mantinea instructs Socrates on the ascent from earthly to transcendent beauty by initiation through love. One comes eventually upon wondrous and transcendent beauty that does not belong to the realm of change, does not wax or wane, that does not correspond to any physical or intellectual object, but rather is "beauty absolute," simple and eternal. This essence of beauty cannot be understood by referent to any aspect of existence, but rather by negation; to be rapt in contemplation of it is to enjoy immortality and to become "the friend of God."[4]

This Platonic tradition of contemplative ascent through initiatory love recurs in later mystical traditions in Sufism and in Christianity. This kind of ascent is not only devotional, though it is that, but also specifically a kind of contemplative ascent through the image of the beloved, at the center of which is transcendence. The lover's longing for the beloved, and the spiritual path through the beloved into the transcendence of self and other is clearly a Platonic theme embedded deep in the dialogues, but it is also visible in the forms of love mysticism we find much later in Sufism and in Christian mysticism.

It is true, of course, that both Sufism and Christian mysticism are profoundly indebted to Platonism. The Platonic tradition was transmitted into Christianity through Dionysius the Areopagite, and later through authors like John Scotus Eriugena, to name only the most influential channels. But we should also recognize that the contemplative ascent through initiatory love that we see in *Phaedrus* and the *Symposium* is beautifully expressed there but does not require Plato's dialogues in order to be rediscovered. Plato's references in his dialogues to ascent through love and beauty refer to an enduring aspect of human inner life that does not require reading the dialogues in order to be rediscovered by the ardent lover. Plato gives expression to what every ardent lover intuitively knows, and what a medieval woman mystic in love with Christ has experienced, too, whether she has heard of Plato or not.

While Plato's dialogues are obviously pagan and polytheistic, they also are not opposed to monotheism in the sense that one god is sometimes referred to in the dialogues as the supreme one, for instance Zeus, of whom all the others are by implication derivative. And the Platonic tradition often refers to τοεν, "the One," which is a metaphysical concept that is not monotheistic but could be interpreted as harmonious with some types of monotheism. Hence Platonism can be imported quite easily into those forms of monotheism that assert, as in Islam or Christianity, a single transcendent deity, less easily into those that posit a personal or tribal god. Without doubt, mysticism in Christianity, and no doubt in other forms of monotheism as well, even if it is not explicit, owes an enormous intellectual debt to Platonism.

The heart of mysticism is the transcendence of subject-object duality, and that is what we find expressed in different ways in Plotinus's extraordinary and virtually inexhaustible exposition in *Enneads*. Whereas in the modern idiom, "mysticism" is often synonymous with "the irrational," Plotinus effortlessly joins reason and its transcendence: he is consummately rational in his efforts to express different facets of what we may term transcendental consciousness. In *Ennead* 5, for instance, he writes about the distinction between "one thing thinking another, and something thinking itself." The latter, he continues, "goes further towards escaping being two."[5] Following the same logic, he continues, "that which is beyond the primary thinking principle will no longer think," because thinking requires an object of thought, hence duality, whereas what is beyond being is also beyond thinking. Perfection and perfect unity/identity is beyond thinking that requires objects of thought. This transcendence is not opposed to thinking; it is not irrational, but it encloses and transcends rationality.

Plotinus also beautifully engages the religious language of the ancient gods to express much the same point. In *Ennead* 5, Plotinus writes about the contemplative ascent to intelligible beauty in terms of ascent to the realm of the gods, among whom Zeus is the most illuminating and beautiful. Zeus, the closest to pure transcendence, illuminates and dazzles everything and everyone, and those who gaze upon him see different facets of his transcendence but all are illumined and transformed by seeing him.[6] What is more, all those who ascend to such beauty and illumination themselves become illumined by it, as if suffused with the red-gold light of a transcendent earth upon which they now walk in the presence of the gods.

And here Plotinus concludes with a key point: for those are not merely spectators of the gods; there is "no longer one thing outside and another outside which is looking at it," for "the keen-sighted has seen [what is] within, although having it, he for the most part does not know he has it." One has the vision of the god in oneself; for this magnificent visionary spectacle does not entail external objects to be perceived; it is, rather, a revelation of what is within, and ultimately it is a revelation not of duality but of unity, of transcendence. This higher reality has its own light, and that light never changes; it is only we who do or do not perceive it and that which it illuminates in the higher, intelligible realm where lives beauty surpassing any earthly beauty.[7] And all of this is within, not outside us; it is more intimate to us than we ourselves.

But the language of the ancient gods is not necessary to express the transcendence to which Plotinus refers, and in fact at other points in the *Enneads* his language, while not monotheistic, nonetheless works both in a pagan and in a Christian context. He writes about transcendence that one should not try to understand it through other things, that is, through similes or metaphors, but should seek to grasp it as it exists in "itself, pure, mixed with nothing, in which all things have a share, though nothing has it."[8] It cannot be measured and "does not come within range of number"; it is not limited; it has no shape, no parts, and no form.[9] He likens this transcendence to participation in the Mystery rites and remarks that "men have forgotten that which from the beginning until now they want and long for."[10] But he also uses theistic language, remarking that "the Good" that "transcends all things" "makes them and lets them exist by themselves, while he remains above them."[11]

Still, neither polytheistic nor theistic language is actually necessary for Plotinus; later in the fifth book, he offers a different analogy. All men, he says, begin with sense perception when they are born, and there are some who during life begin to awaken to what is above the sensory. But there is "a third kind of godlike men who by their greater power and the sharpness of their eyes" are raised above the clouds, "overlooking all things here below," and "delighting in the true region which is their own, like a man who has come home after a long wandering to his own well-ordered country."[12] And what is this region of which Plotinus writes? It is beauty, and wisdom, but these are characteristics or expressions of it. In essence, it is "true Intellect."[13] This Intellect is beyond the soul, beyond being; and since it "possesses itself in peace, is everlasting fullness."[14]

The Platonic tradition as represented in the work of Plato and Plotinus—as well as Proclus, Porphyry, Iamblichus, Damascius, and others in this lineage—is not philosophical in the modern sense of discursive analytical disputation, but rather represents the headwaters for what in Christianity becomes known, broadly speaking, as mysticism. Of course Platonism expresses itself through discursive exposition—no doubt of that. So too, often, do mystics. But the discursive exposition of a Plotinus, for instance, is not an end in itself; it is rather at the service of the contemplative ascent and transcendence, as is clear in these passages from Plotinus's *Enneads.* The word "mysticism" in this context refers to the contemplative ascent from a condition of perceived duality (divided subject and object) and suffering, to the transcendence of duality or subject/object division, and a concomitant beatitude or joy. This ascent is clearly there in Plato's dialogues, especially *Phaedrus* and *Symposium*, as also in Plotinus, and in the many mystics who belong to the broader current of Christian Platonism.

The headwaters of this tradition are to be found in the works of Dionysius the Areopagite, who probably lived in the fifth century

AD, but about whose identity there is still much speculation and little certainty, even with regard to which century he belongs. There are, of course, others whose work is also important to understanding subsequent mysticism in the Christian tradition—one thinks here of Origen, Clement of Alexandria, Evagrius Ponticus, and the Desert Fathers, for instance. All of these are important in different ways for understanding mysticism as it develops through subsequent centuries. Clement of Alexandria, for instance, distinguished an authentic Christian gnosis from false gnosis, hence providing a precedent for understanding a current within Christianity as having gnostic insight at its center. But among the many important figures during the early period of Christianity, Dionysius the Areopagite remains essential for contextualizing and understanding subsequent currents of mysticism.

That Dionysius's works belong to the larger current of Platonism, but diverted into Christianity, can hardly be gainsaid. There are, of course, differences, as indeed there are major distinctions to be made between Platonists proper. Just as Proclus, Porphyry, and Iamblichus are each distinctive, so too each of them is distinct from Dionysius. Whereas all Platonists properly speaking are pagan, Dionysius is incontrovertibly Christian, and his subsequent influence on mystics in both the West and the East is vast. What makes Dionysius so remarkable is that he preserves essential elements of Platonism, but in a new Christian theological context.

It is not to give enough recognition to Dionysius's achievement, though, to say only that he preserved the essential elements of Platonism, for what he also did was synthesize Platonism in a way that provides a contextual framework for all of Christian mysticism. Central among these is the Dionysian concepts of *via positiva* and *via negativa*, or kataphatic and apophatic mysticism, the notion of ascent through contemplation of symbols or images (that which is posited) and the notion of ascent through negation of all sensory or conceptual attributions. Also essential is the concept of hierarchy in the celestial realms, mirrored in the ecclesiastical hierarchy. For Dionysius, the ecclesiastical hierarchy is not a matter of clerical positions, but of gnostic illumination—those who are above are the initiators of and channels of divine grace for those below them. These two aspects—contemplative ascent and the descent of divine grace through initiation—are of course complementary and distinctively expressed in the Dionysian synthesis.

Dionysius expresses his gratitude to his own illuminated teacher, Hierotheus (revealer of divinity), thus indicating that he belongs to an initiatory lineage himself, and by implication, by reading his treatises we are ourselves initiated into the lineage too. In this way, Dionysius (like Clement of Alexandria and some others) creates a space for an authentically gnostic dimension and lineage at the center of Christianity. In fact, if one accepts the Dionysian body of work as a whole, then one is effectively centering Christianity not on belief or articles of faith, but on direct inner knowledge and illumination. This esoteric understanding of Christianity is the basis for Christian mysticism.

But aren't only theistic, dualistic, exoteric forms of Christianity "orthodox"? To answer this question, we have to recognize that from at least the time of the Nicene Creed (381 AD) on, much of what we currently understand as Christianity, particularly in the West, in actuality has been exoteric, that is, consisting primarily in professions of faith or belief around which are bodies of accumulated doctrines in which one also has to profess belief in order to be a member. Exoteric Christianity is, in its very nature, dualistic, in that it posits an eternal separation between the believer and his God, often presented as a deity with whom one has a personal relationship. The monotheistic God, in the more extreme forms of exoteric religion, is seen as separated not only from believers, but from the world as well. The afterlife is also largely conceived in bifurcated terms of heaven and hell. And many of those from such a perspective would say that only exoteric forms of Christianity are orthodox. Indeed, in the contemporary world, that only exoteric Christianity exists is in fact true for most people. Dionysius the Areopagite and the tradition of Platonic mysticism simply do not exist for the vast majority of Christians, including theologians.

However, the tradition of Platonic mysticism does in fact exist. As Willigis Jäger points out, Plato "played a definitive role in the West in creating a non-theistic theology." Plato, Jäger adds, "does not recognize an ontological dualism, despite all the false intepretations of his writings." Platonism actually survived not in philosophy, Jäger writes, but "in mysticism, to be more accurate." He mentions Proclus, Plotinus, Evagrius, Meister Eckhart, and Nicholas of Cusa as examples of the tradition of Platonic mysticism, and in fact Jäger is absolutely right on all counts.[15] What is more, Jäger is a contemporary exemplar of this tradition himself.

What distinguishes the tradition of Platonic mysticism, just as Jäger observes, is that "matter . . . only becomes reality through the timeless ideas manifested in it," that there is "no dividing gap between

God and the world, that the world is no less than the revelation of the divine," and what is more, that salvation can be understood as "awakening to our actual essence." Salvation, in this tradition, is realization of the divine.[16] And the divine is not separate from us or from our world, nor could it be or we could not realize it for ourselves. These aspects of Platonic mysticism are its vital center, manifested above all in the transcendent illumination of consciousness that we may call a mystical breakthrough. This breakthrough is directly described in Dionysius the Areopagite's *Mystical Theology* as the negation of all posited concepts, indeed of all sensory, bodily, or mental phenomena.

The broader medieval mystical tradition must be understood in this Dionysian context, which is to say, ultimately in a Platonic context. Some scholars claim that Dionysius is, in one aspect or another, not really Platonic, or that in some respects that he broke with Platonism. However, I have yet to discover where, in essential ways, such claims are entirely convincing. To give an example: Vladimir Lossky held, and others have accepted that Dionysius broke definitively with the Neoplatonic conception of hierarchy, as well as with the Neoplatonic emanationist cosmology. Perhaps this is so in both cases. But it is also true that Dionysius is author of *The Celestial Hierarchy* and of *Ecclesiastical Hierarchy*, neither of which can be said to repudiate concepts of hierarchy—quite the opposite. Lossky wants Dionysius to have refused to let Neoplatonic philosophy dominate the Christian mystery, and there might be some truth in this.[17] But Platonism has its mysteries too, which were shared with Christianity through the works of Dionysius; in his work, Platonism and Christianity, and their mysteries, are fused.[18] The genius of Dionysius was to accomplish this fusion in a way that preserves the mysteries of both.

What Dionysius provides is foundation for what is now known as the history of Christian mysticism, but in fact is a chapter in the history of Platonism—hence my term "Platonic mysticism." In Dionysius we find the *ur*-formulation of kataphatic and apophatic mysticism—that is, the complementaries of ascent through images (*via positive* or kataphatic mysticism), and of ascent through negation (*via positiva* or apophatic mysticism. Apophatic mysticism is, of course, essential because as the negation of all conceptual and perceptual attributions, it is the transcendence of ordinary or discursive consciousness, the sign and seal of this tradition of Platonic mysticism. It is central to the Platonic tradition as represented in Plotinus and Damascius, and it is central to Dionysius's work as evidenced in his *Mystical Theology*, from which it then manifests throughout the subsequent history of Christian mysticism in such well-known and lesser-known figures as John Scotus Eriugena, Robert Grosseteste, Thomas Gallus, Meister Eckhart, Jan van Ruysbroek, Johannes Tauler, Marguerite Porete, Jean Gerson, Nicholas of Cusa, the English author of *The Cloud of Unknowing*, the author of the *Theologia Germanica*, Marsilio Ficino, Pico della Mirandola, and Giordano Bruno, Jacob Böhme, Henry More, Ralph Cudworth, Thomas Traherne, Ralph Waldo Emerson, William Ralph Inge, Nicholas Berdyaev, Bernadette Roberts, and Willigis Jäger.

Platonic contextualization is so important because it reveals that the history of Christian mysticism is not one of discontinuity alone, but also of continuity. Often Christian mysticism is portrayed as discontinuous in its history, and of course there is some truth in this. For instance, it would seem that a figure like Eckhart emerges almost *ex nihilo*, and bears little or no links to his Platonic sources, let alone to Gnostic ones in antiquity. In fact, I coined the term "ahistorical continuity" in order to describe this phenomenon.[19] But all the same, there is continuity in the history of mysticism, and it is provided by Platonic mysticism, in particular by the complementary unity of kataphatic and apophatic mysticism rooted in the Dionysian fusion of Platonism and Christianity, which opens space within the Christian tradition for a contemplative or gnostic path independent of specific doctrinal constructs.

What is more, the two complementary approaches of *via positiva* and *via negativa* allow us to see that types of mysticism often presented as fundamentally different—for instance, visionary mysticism as opposed to a mysticism of transcendence—can be seen as complementary and related to the extent that "behind" visions is the background of sheer transcendence of subject and object to which the vision is potentially an introduction. Of course, some visions might in fact be delusional, hallucinatory, or even deranged—attributable to the malign inspiration of the devil or to demons, to put it in religious rather than psychological terms. Nonetheless, what Dionysius provides is at least the possibility that both visionary and transcendent paths might be ascents toward the same ultimate transcendence of subject and object.

Dionysius's fusion of Platonic mysticism was channeled into Western Christianity through various figures, seminal among which was John Scotus Eriugena. But Eriugena was far from alone in the effort to make Dionysius's work available in Western Europe. Dionysius's work, brought to the French monastery of Saint-Denis in 827, was translated by its Abbot, Hilduin, then translated again by John Scotus Eriugena, who went on to write his masterwork, *Periphyseon*, which is infused with Dionsyian Platonism. Dionysius's work was translated anew by John of Sarracen and provided a commentary by Anastasius, a librarian in Paris; and the most essential work of Dionysius, *Mystical Theology*, was translated and provided another set of glosses and commentary by Thomas Gallus and Robert Grosseteste, Bishop of Lincoln, again in the thirteenth century.[20]

Among all of the authors inspired by Dionysius, however, one of the most important and instructive is Nicholas of Cusa (1401–1464), who in 1448 was given the title and position of cardinal in the Catholic Church by Pope Nicholas V. Since Nicholaus Cusanus (as he was known in Latin) was an influential member of the Roman Catholic ecclesiastical hierarchy, a bishop and later cardinal, he clearly was not at odds with the Church. Nicholas's primary insight, expressed in different ways in his numerous written works, letters, and sermons, including his most well-known treatise, *De Docta Ignorantia* (*On Learned Ignorance*), as well as works like *Idiota de Sapientia* (*The Layman [Idiot] on Wisdom*), *De Visione Dei* (*On the Vision of God*), or *De Apice Theoriae* (*The Apex of Contemplation*), was that transcendence is beyond our concepts, categories, or terms—it cannot be captured by them.

Hence Nicholas emphasizes a new *via*, beyond the *via positiva* and *via negativa*, the *via superexcellentiae*, or way of sheer or absolute transcendence. By it, Nicholas underscores the absolutely transcendent and incomprehensible nature of God, which cannot be grasped by human reason or perception. The divine nature is supersensible, superintelligible, beyond all that we can characterize it as, even through superlatives. This *via superexcellentiae* is even beyond the coincidence of opposites (*coincidentia oppositorum*).[21] It requires us to engage in an intellective, mystical leap, for "in sensible things we shall contemplate intellectual things," and we ascend by a certain unproportionality from "transitory and fleeting temporality" "to eternity," characterized by "a steadfast permanence of rest."[22]

Of course, there is a certain paradox here, for it would seem that the *via superexcellentiae*, with its assertion that mystical recognition of the divine takes place in the absence of both attribution (it is x or it is *like* x: the kataphatic way) and refusal of attribution (it is not x or it is not like x: the apophatic way) is actually a different expression of the apophatic or negative way. In this light, the *via superexcellentiae* is really not other than the *via negativa*, expressed in a way that underscores its refusal of any conceptual or perceptual framework for illuminative or transcendent understanding.

Such transcendence is attained, Nicholas tells us, through "sacred ignorance," meaning that God is ineffable, greater than anything expressible through words, and "as incomprehensible to creatures as infinite light is to darkness."[23] In a letter to Cardinal Julian, Nicholas wrote about his personal experience of sacred ignorance, observing that only when returning "by sea from Greece," he was offered a gift by "the Father of Lights" to "transcend those perennial truths that can be reached by reason."[24] The letter makes clear, if it is not clear enough from the text, that Nicholas directly experienced that about which he wrote, and it is certainly significant that the experience took place on his return from Greece, home of Platonism.

What we find, when we dig more deeply into the history of mysticism, is that throughout is woven the red thread of Platonism, and in particular, of the sheer transcendence that is at the center of the work of Plotinus and of Damascius, as well as of Dionysius the Areopagite's *Mystical Theology*. This is the key to understanding mysticism, whether it is in the work of Meister Eckhart, or Johannes Tauler, or for that matter, of poor Marguerite Porete, the author of the beautiful and uncompromising *Mirror of Simple Souls*. Forbidden to share her work or her mystical understanding, on 1 June 1310, condemned by the Inquisition as heretical, Marguerite was burned to death in Paris. And at the center of her work, just as at the center of Eckhart's and Tauler's for that matter, was the recognition that the illuminated soul "is nothing, for she sees her nothingness by means of the abundance of divine Understanding, which makes her nothing and places her in nothingness. And so she is all things. . . . without bottom. One does not find oneself who cannot attain this."[25] In such passages we recognize, once again, the key: apophatic mysticism in the tradition of Dionysius.[26]

It is worth reflecting for a moment on why Nicholas of Cusa could rise to the level of a cardinal in the church, while Marguerite Porete could be burned to death in Paris. Some authors see in her work a feminine, visionary mysticism interested in gender balance in the deity, and it is indeed probable that she was burned in part because she was a woman mystic whose work challenged the Church's male hierarchy. Eckhart, Tauler, and Cusanus all tacked closer to orthodoxy than Marguerite, whose work in its espousal of mystical freedom implicitly does challenge the hierarchic authority of the Church and its doctrines. But at heart, her work was in many respects quite well aligned with that of other experiential mystical works in the English, French, and German traditions.[27] To put it succinctly, the individual inclinations and situations of mystics may put them on one side or the other of putative orthodoxy, but that does not affect their collective indebtedness to the Platonic-Dionysian tradition of apophatic mysticism.

When we turn to the tradition of English mysticism, we also find this profound indebtedness to the apophatic tradition, particularly in *The Cloud of Unknowing.* In his preface to *The Cloud of Unknowing,* Simon Tugwell situates this little treatise of advice on the contemplative path as squarely in the tradition of Proclus, Dionysius, and Eckhart, that is as Platonic. It is Platonic not explicitly, he writes, so much as in spirit. There is in us something that draws us higher, that pulls us inward, which Plato expressed in terms of the erotic ascent of the lover toward the divine beloved, and which the author of *The Cloud* expresses as the inner desire of the soul to be united with God. Tugwell writes that "the author of *The Cloud* is clearly dependent, however loosely, on the Platonist tradition that our minds are defeated when we try to draw close to God; only love can take the final step, drawing us into the dark yet dazzling mystery of God as he is in himself."[28] There are two aspects of the Platonic tradition visible in *The Cloud,* then: the attractive power of uniting with the divine, and the dark transcendence of the union itself.

Near the conclusion of *The Cloud of Unknowing,* the author exhorts us to "leave aside this everywhere and this everything, in exchange for this nowhere and this nothing." We should not care if our senses do not understand it, because in fact it is "so worthy a thing in itself" that sensory-based consciousness cannot recognize its inestimable value. It is dark seen from outside, but it is in truth an "abundance of spiritual light." Only the outward or exoteric man calls it nothing, for the inward or esoteric knower recognizes that it is in fact "All."[29] Embedded in this little treatise of direct contemplative advice is clear evidence of the Dionysian tradition, and in particular of how we are to transcend the realm of senses and objectifying discursive reason by our profound inner "work . . . in this nothing and this nowhere."[30]

We are emphasizing the Platonic-Dionysian tradition in Christian mysticism in this brief survey not because it corresponds to all forms of mysticism, but because it has insufficiently been recognized to what extent this tradition exists within the history of Christian mysticism. It is obvious that *The Cloud of Unknowing* and related treatises of English mysticism offering advice to the contemplative practitioner owe their very existence to the prior tradition of Christian Platonism that is central to the Dionysian current. That Platonism more broadly is essential to the work and thought of many figures, including Ficino and Pico of the Italian Renaissance, is also obvious, but our purpose here is not to survey every single figure so much as to demonstrate the existence and explanatory importance of the Platonic-Dionysian current for understanding mysticism.

At first glance, it might seem that mysticism disappears around the beginning of what has become known as the modern era, but it was already dwindling by the seventeenth century and the rise of materialism, rationalism, and Cartesian dualism, well before the nineteenth and twentieth centuries. And indeed there is some truth to the view that mysticism not just wanes, but disappears with the onset of modernity. Nonetheless, there are major counterfigures to this tendency, and here I want to look at just a few of them. The first of these is the group known as the Cambridge Platonists, in England in the seventeenth century.

The Cambridge Platonists are sometimes mischaracterized; it is relatively rare for them to be placed in the category of mysticism. But it is by no means unheard of, and in fact, I would argue, that is where some, and perhaps most or even all of them belong. The group included Benjamin Whichcote (1609–1683), Ralph Cudworth (1617–1688), Peter Sterry (1613–1672), John Smith (1618–1652), Nathaniel Culverwell (1619–1651), John Worthington (1618–1671), Anne Conway (1630–1679), and John Norris (1657–1711). But of the Cambridge Platonists, I would emphasize just two: Henry More (1614–1687) and John Smith (1618–1652). Without doubt many of these figures, but above all Henry More and John Smith, represent the intersection of Platonism and mysticism.

The Cambridge Platonists as a group represented an English Renaissance on their own, at least as much as earlier figures like Marsilio Ficino and Pico della Mirandola represented and inspired an Italian Renaissance, that is, a strong reaffirmation of Platonism not just as if it were sterile analytical philosophical discourse, but as a lived reality. George Panichas described the Cambridge Platonists this way: "Cambridge Platonism represents the quintessence of religious mysticism in the seventeenth century."[31] It was a "revival of the Greek spirit, especially as found in the thought of Plato and in the [N]eoplatonic thought of Plotinus." Uninterested in mechanism or materialism, the Cambridge Platonists sought instead—despite living in an era of terrific religious "narrowness and bigotry"—"communion with the Mind of God." They "sought to climb the spiritual ladder from earth to heaven" through "the purgative, illuminative, and unitive states of divine being."[32]

Henry More was the most mystical of the Cambridge Platonists precisely because he belonged to the Platonic-Plotinian tradition. More affirmed, directly against the emergence of modern materialism and atheism, the possibility of mystical union of the soul with God.[33] As Robert Crocker put it, "More, from the perspective of his mystical Platonism, believed that while most Christians were to a greater or lesser extent inspired by God in their thoughts and actions, the possibility of a real and substantial union between the soul and God ('deification') was the neglected cornerstone of orthodox theology."[34] This union is possible because, as More put it in his *An Antidote Against Atheism*, "It remains therefore undeniable that there is an inseparable Idea of a Being absolutely Perfect ever residing, though not always acting, in the Soul of Man."[35] More had experienced this for himself, and was, according to his early biographer, "once Ten Days together, nowhere (as he termed it), or in one continued fit of contemplation."[36] More's life, says Panichas, was "a long contemplation, a life of unbroken prayer."[37]

Another of the Cambridge Platonists who represents well the category of Platonic mystic was John Smith, about whom Frederick Powicke writes that he was a "spiritual genius."[38] Smith too followed Plato and Plotinus, insisting that the "true metaphysical or contemplative man," "abstracting himself from himself, endeavours the nearest union with the Divine essence that may be . . . knitting his own centre, if he have any, into the centre of Divine being."[39] This union takes place through an inner leap, "shooting up above" one's "logical or self-rational life." Smith writes that attaining divine knowledge is best understood as coming not through "Verbal description" but through "Spiritual sensation." He refers to Plotinus's remark that the eye cannot perceive the sun unless it becomes sunlike (*Ennead* I.6.9) and remarks that likewise neither can man behold God unless he becomes godlike.[40]

Smith, like More, was revered by his friends and colleagues as exemplary in his demeanor and conduct, but also as someone who had directly realized for himself that of which he wrote. It was said that More had had an illuminative experience that lasted ten days and that both he and Smith were renowned for their kindness and gentility. This corresponds to what Smith wrote in "The Excellency and Nobleness of True Religion," that "the first Propertie and Effect of True Religion whereby it expresses its own Nobleness is this, That it widens and enlarges all the faculties of the Soul, and begets a true Ingenuity, Liberty, and Amplitude, the most free and Generous Spirit, in the Minds of Good men."[41] "True Religion," he continues with the assurance of someone who knew this directly, "is indeed no Art, but an inward Nature that contains all the laws and measures of its motion within it self."[42] Smith's is a Platonic Christian mysticism in which "[t]he nearer any Being comes to God, who is that Infinite fullness that fills all in all, the more vast and large and unbounded it is; as the further it slides from him, the more it is streightned and confined, as Plato has long since concluded."[43]

The Cambridge Platonists existed, after all, in a context of developing scientific materialism, but represented a full-on assault against materialism and in favor of religion as inner life. They also represented a clear alternative to confessionally based Protestantism of the time that could be quite puritanical, ideological, and antimystical. The Cambridge Platonists, and in particular More and Smith, demonstrate the possibility of a Platonic renaissance in the context of English Protestantism at the beginning of modernity, but they also demonstrate that Platonism could recur in many contexts. They spoke for an experiential path carried on by many thousands of souls in the Christian tradition.

After the Cambridge Platonists, arguably the most influential exponent of Platonic mysticism was Ralph Waldo Emerson, who in his first book, *Nature*, asked, "[S]hould not we have a poetry and philosophy of insight, and not of tradition, and a religion by revelation to us, and not the history of theirs?"[44] In other words, Emerson was asking, do we not have the faculty of direct insight ourselves? Why should we rely only on the insight of others, recorded in histories? In *Nature*, Emerson insists that we see ourselves in relation to nature and to the divine, *now*, and for ourselves, and that we not merely grope through the "dry bones of the past." Nature here "refers to essences unchanged by man; space, the air, the river, the leaf." The term "essences," here, is reminiscent of Plato's Forms or Ideas; and indeed Plato is visible throughout the work as a recurrent subtext.

But Emerson's clearest manifestation of Platonic mysticism in *Nature* is the famous passage in which Emerson alludes to his "standing on bare ground" "uplifted into infinite space," become a "transparent eyeball," in which "I am nothing. I see all. The currents of the Universal Being circulate through me; I am part or particle of God."[45] Emerson also wants to remark on his "greatest delight" in the next paragraph, which manifests itself in "an occult relation between man and the vegetable." For, he continues, "they nod to me and I to them." And in the third paragraph, he remarks, "the power to produce this delight, does not reside in nature, but in man, or in a harmony of both."[46]

The last three sections of *Nature* are devoted to describing how we gain access to direct spiritual insight. The chapter "Idealism" outlines how "nature is made to conspire with spirit to emancipate us."[47] In "Spirit," Emerson emphasizes the immediacy of transcendence. We can realize that

> the highest is present to the soul of man, that the dread universal essence, which is not wisdom, or love, or beauty, or power, but all in one, and each entirely, is that for which all things exist, and that by which they are; that spirit creates; that behind nature, through nature, spirit is present; that spirit is one and not compound; that spirit does not act upon us from without, that is, in space and time, but spiritually, or through ourselves. Therefore, that spirit, that is, the Supreme Being, does not build up nature around us, but puts it forth through us, as the life of the tree puts forth new branches and leaves through the pores of the old.[48]

Emerson, he tells us, is pointing toward

> The golden key
> Which opes the palace of eternity.[49]

This key is the "view" toward which he is pointing.

In the final chapter, "Prospects," Emerson recapitulates his Platonic manifesto. He remarks that "the highest reason is always the truest" and that the most refined truth may seem dim only because it resides deepest in the mind "among the eternal verities." Empirical science in fact can "cloud the sight" because the categorizing, rationalistic faculty actually blocks out the "*metaphysics*" of nature, and "a certain occult recognition and sympathy."[50]

Emerson encourages us to awaken our higher reason, like a banished king who vaults at once into his throne. Hence he also refers to "Reason's momentary grasp of the sceptre; the exertions of a power which exists not in time or space, but an instantaneous in-streaming causing power." Reason is not rationality, but the faculty that perceives transcendence; it is the "king" that vaults at once into the throne of unity. At once, Emerson concludes, "shall we come to look at the world with new eyes." With this realization, one enters a dominion "such as now is beyond [one's] dream of God," and with the wonder of a "blind man" who is gradually restored to "perfect sight."[51]

Emerson's Platonic mysticism is visible in his other works, as I detailed in *American Gurus* (2014). In particular, his famous essay "The Over-Soul" is about how time and eternity intersect, for "within man is the soul of the whole; the wise silence; the universal beauty, to which every part and particle is equally related; the eternal ONE." What is more, the soul is "not a faculty, but a light," and "from within or from behind, a light shines through us upon things, and makes us aware that we are nothing, but the light is all."[52] Here, as in *Nature*, Emerson is asserting the transcendence of self and the recognition of Plotinian insight.

Here too, Emerson writes, "The soul's advances are not made by gradation, such as can be represented by motion in a straight line; but rather by ascension of state. . . . The growths of genius are of a certain *total* character."[53] In fact, "with each divine impulse the mind rends the thin rinds of the visible and finite, and comes out into eternity, and inspires and expires its air." For "Omniscience flows into the intellect, and makes what we call genius."[54] "Genius," he writes, is not merely talent or intellectual gifts; "genius is religious."

Emerson's direct assertion of Platonic mysticism was precisely what incensed his critics. In "The Latest Form of Infidelity," his response to Emerson's *Divinity School Address*, Andrews Norton said, "I know of no absolute certainty beyond the limit of momentary consciousness; a certainty that vanishes the instant it exists, and is lost in the region of metaphysical doubt." For someone like Norton, "there can be no intuition, no direct perception of the truth of Christianity, no metaphysical certainty." And another critic insisted censoriously "the doctrine that the mind possesses a faculty of intuitively discovering the truths of religion, is . . . utterly untenable."[55] For "consciousness or intuition can inform us of nothing but what exists in our own minds."[56]

What we see in the sharp contrast between Emerson and his critics is the age-old opposition between Platonic mysticism and materialist dogmatism. This polarization is visible in the medieval era—one thinks of the Inquisition on the one side and figures such as Giordano Bruno on the other—but it becomes dominant in the modern era. Already in the period of the Cambridge Platonists it was emerging, becoming clearer in the time of Emerson, but by the late twentieth century, what B. Alan Wallace terms dogmatic scientific materialism had become the dominant mode of thought, so much so that Platonism and its modern offspring, Transcendentalism, by and large were eclipsed in the academic world. What incensed Andrews Norton about Emerson in the nineteenth century was no doubt profoundly irritating to scientific materialists of the late twentieth or twenty-first centuries as well: the assertion of the possibilities of direct spiritual insight.

Although Platonism as such largely disappeared from the surface of modern intellectual life, it remained alive underground, sometimes appearing in disguise. In academic philosophy departments, Plato and above all Neoplatonism were almost completely excluded in favor of analytical or other forms of philosophy that supremely privileged discursive reason while by and large dismissing out of hand religious or metaphysical traditions. In the broader Western intellectual world, Platonism was presented in bizarrely distorted forms, as "dualism," or as nascent "totalitarianism," but mostly was excluded and ignored. Still, because it is the core intellectual force behind and metaphysical context for understanding the West, Platonic mysticism did not disappear but appeared in new, sometimes altered forms.

One form it took, for instance, was in psychology, in the works and thought of Carl Jung. In *The Darkening Spirit*, David Tacey writes at length about the response to Carl Jung in the academic world. He draws on a term coined by John Carroll, "pneumaphobia," by which he means a pathological fear of the spirit (Greek: pneuma). "The phobic response," Tacey observes, "is evident in the knee-jerk responses to Jung as a 'mystic' or 'religious'—terms that are seen as abusive and damning."[57] He goes on to write, "Critics who charged Jung with 'mysticism' were partly right, I believe, but underestimated the importance of the mystical in human experience and the development of consciousness."[58]

Jung's work is not exactly in the tradition of Platonic mysticism, but it certainly was influenced by it. David Tacey refers to the "offence of the archetypes" as particularly egregious for many scholars and points out that Jung's notion of archetypes owes more than a little to Platonic ideas or forms. Tacey points out that for Jung, "[a]rchetypes 'in themselves' are unknowable and regarded as transcendental factors . . . in the manner of Platonic 'ideas.'" Jung thus represents, in his use of concepts like the "numinous" archetypes, "what Eliade calls a 'new humanism,' that is, one who restores a traditional view of the world and places spirit [in this case archetypes or Platonic ideas], not man, at the centre of things. The secular mind becomes phobic whenever its freedom is compromised."[59]

Jung's work and thought contain many inventions and new aspects that were part of his life's mission to recognize and understand psychological forces at work beneath the surface of an apparently placid modernity. His notion of the "unconscious," his emphasis on dreams and on the forces at work in them, and his view of the ancient gods as living archetypes may indeed be offensive to a modern materialistic mindset, and if so, are so because they hark back to the Platonic and ancient religious traditions in which the gods were living realities. Among Jung's insights was to see that when we do not recognize but suppress our inner life, its forces lash out, and hence we have the conflagrations of the early and mid twentieth century, the world wars.

Another such figure whose work can be better understood in light of Platonic mysticism is Mircea Eliade, who in the midtwentieth century was the dominant figure in the then-nascent field of religious studies. The extent to which Eliade's work manifests a Platonic origin is not often recognized; his work, if taught at all, is typically taught as part of the history of the study of religion, but in isolation from his work's Platonic precedent and origin. It became *de rigueur* to attack Eliade as an "essentialist" or to use an even more ridiculous term, a "religionist," a "religionist" being anyone who takes seriously the philosophical and religious perspectives that he or she is studying.[60] But Eliade's work does not exist on its own, separate from the Western philosophico-religious tradition; it is a continuation of it.

Eliade's model for religion emphasizes the timelessness at the center of religious experience. He was, as a young man, a practitioner of yoga in India, and he drew his mysticism from that experience and from the Platonic tradition. He makes this clear in a number of works, among them *Myths, Dreams, and Mysteries*, where he outlines again how the purpose of religious life is to attain "to the Timeless," that is, to the "eternal present which preceded the temporal experience inaugurated by the 'fall' into human existence." "In other words," he continues, "it is possible, starting from any moment of temporal duration, to exhaust that duration by retracing its course to the source and so come out into the Timeless, into eternity. But that is to transcend the human condition and to regain the non-conditioned state, which preceded the fall into Time and the wheel of existences."[61] What Eliade outlines here, and at many points in his work, is a lucid, very simplified theory of mysticism.

And Eliade makes clear that his theory of mysticism has Pythagorean and Platonic precedent. In particular, he refers to the Platonic tradition of *anamnesis*, that is, of remembering one's transcendent origins (literally, "not-forgetting"). Eliade writes that "it is in the Platonic doctrine of the Remembrance of impersonal realities that we find the most astonishing persistence of archaic thought." The Platonic "doctrine of Ideas," he continues, "renewed and re-valorized the archaic and universal myth of a fabulous, pleromatic *illud tempus*, which man has to remember is he is to know the *truth* and participate in *Being*."[62] The italics are in the original. Eliade adds as a gloss, "In Plato it is only the pre-existence of the soul in the timeless universe of Ideas that matters; and the *truth* (*aletheia*) is the remembrance of that impersonal situation."[63]

And Eliade does not conclude there. He refers instead to the modern inclination of academics, derived from a largely unconscious inheritance from Judaism and Christianity of materialistic historicism and a tyranny of linear time. Much in the vein of his colleague at the Eranos conferences, Henry Corbin, Eliade observes that the prevailing historicization of scholarship means that meaning and transcendence are often excluded; time is documented in detail, but timelessness, traditionally expressed through myth and ritual, is in the modern context often ignored. Eliade is mild in what he writes, compared certainly to his colleague Corbin's denunciation of secular historicism and insistence on the vital importance of transcendence and timelessness for what it means to be human.[64] And the key to recovering mythological keys to timeless reality is, Eliade tells us, *anamnesis*, that is, Platonic remembering that opens into "primordial Time, the Time in which men established their cultural behavior patterns."[65]

When Eliade explains the nature and importance of myths, it is clear that he is doing so from a Platonic perspective. He writes, "Myths are the most general and effective means of awakening and maintaining consciousness of another world, a beyond, whether it be the divine world or the world of the Ancestors. This 'other world' represents a superhuman, 'transcendent' plane, the plane of *absolute realities*." Through the experience of the sacred transcendent, he continues, "the ideas of *reality*, *truth*, and *significance* first dawn."[66] In other words, myth celebrated through ritual offers the opportunity for the human to touch or experience transcendent reality, the timeless realm of Ideas or Archetypes. Myth is "recollection" (remembering, *anamnesis*) "of the primordial event." Eliade emphasizes that what is experienced in mythic reality is transmundane truth, absolute reality that in turn shapes and guides us in how we make our way in the fleeting world of shadows.[67]

What's more, Eliade was part of a larger scholarly community during the apex of his life, which also had an interesting and little-known Platonic connection. This community, which met in Ascona, Switzerland, organized and sponsored by the remarkable Olga Fröbe, was called "Eranos." It included among its presenters not only Eliade, but Jung, Scholem, Corbin, and many others, and the story of this remarkable venue for scholarship on religion, unmatched before or since, is told in H. T. Hakl's *Eranos: An Intellectual Alternative History of the Twentieth Century*. What is less known than Eranos itself—commemorated in the series of Bollingen volumes drawn from the conference papers—is that the Eranos group actually formally merged with another effort to restore a Platonic Academy in Europe during the 1950s. This effort was led by Walter Robert Corti, who saw Eranos "as being in the tradition of the Platonic Academy, which he deemed to be the 'highest form and eternal model of all sodalities, whether education or involving a shared way of life."[68] Corti gave a paper at Eranos on the history of the Platonic Academy, and he sought to make of Eranos and this new Platonic Academy "an academy of the spirit" that could remedy the errors of the age.[69] In this context, even though in the end the merger between Eranos and the Platonic Academy did not work out, we can see the Platonic cast of later descriptions of Eranos as representing and providing a venue for "das Übergeschichtliche" (that which transcends history), that is, for "hierophanies" in which the eternal is revealed.[70]

At this juncture, we need to recognize the role that Asian religions, and in particular Hinduism and Buddhism, began to play in the West already in the nineteenth century with Emerson and even before him. I discussed this subject in some detail in *American Transcendentalism and Asian Religions*, so I'm not going to repeat what is already there.[71] But it is important, in discussing mysticism in the twentieth and twenty-first centuries, to recognize that mystics living in the present day for the most part are influenced by Asian religious traditions. For someone like Meister Eckhart, living in medieval Germany, Buddhism effectively did not exist. But were he born in North America in the twenty-first century, Buddhism clearly would exist in his world, and a contemporary Eckhart almost certainly could not be understood without reference to it.

Already Eliade, as a young man, had gone to India and directly studied yoga, which in turn was pivotal for his subsequent writing. That said, his mode of expression remained Platonic: looking back into Western cultural history, he found in Platonic language the best way to understand and convey the nature of religion and of religious experience, especially ritual, myth, and transcendence. These two aspects of Eliade's work cannot ultimately be separated, nor can they be for virtually any mystic of the midtwentieth century onward. Franklin Merrell-Wolff (1887–1985) for instance, was inspired by Shankaracarya and Vedanta, as well as by Buddhism but can be compared to Plotinus; and even the Roman Catholic mystic Bernadette Roberts (b. 1931) refers to Buddhism in her account of her awakening to "no-self," taking pains to distinguish her insights from those of Vedanta.[72] In fact, arguably the most important development in Christian practice during the twentieth and twenty-first centuries was the advent, in the West, of Buddhism and Hinduism, but particularly of Buddhism.

What makes Buddhism in particular so influential is that it provides multiple traditions of meditation training and practice, as well as terminological and cartological structure for understanding the mind, the path toward awakening, and the nature of awakening. As a result, it offers natural complements for understanding and expressing Western contemplative practices and traditions, and the truth is, hardly any work of mysticism or on mysticism today or from the recent past can be understood without recognizing its often hidden or partially hidden antecedents in Asian religions, and especially in Buddhism.

There are a number of Roman Catholic priests who went through Zen Buddhist training sufficient to become teachers in that tradition but who retained their Catholic tradition and identity as well. Some examples include Patrick Hawk, a Catholic priest and Zen teacher whose training was with Robert Aitken Roshi; Robert E. Kennedy, a Catholic priest and Zen teacher who heads the Morning Star Zendo in New Jersey and author of *Zen Spirit, Christian Spirit*;[73] and William Johnston, author of *Christian Zen* and other books;[74] but most important for us is Willigis Jäger, a German Roman Catholic monk who trained in Japan in the Sanbo Kyodan tradition, was recognized as a roshi or teacher in it, and who later founded his own Zen-Christian lineage, that of the *Leere Wolke*, or "Empty Cloud."

Jäger is the most important figure not only (at least arguably) in the fusion of Roman Catholic mysticism and Zen Buddhism, but also in the development of what he terms a global "transconfessional" spirituality. He created a foundation or *stiftung* in Germany, the *West-Östliche Weisheit* or *West-Eastern Wisdom*, and helped found a number of centers in Europe, as well as train and recognize a number of spiritual teachers in his East-West lineage. His lineage and teaching, while drawing on his Zen Buddhist training and his Benedictine practice, have their origin explicitly in the Platonic *philosophia perennis* expressed in contemporary terms as "integrated thinking and action" or "integrated spirituality."[75]

Jäger's transconfessional spirituality based in Zen and Catholicism developed over time. In his earlier books, like *The Way to Contemplation* and *Contemplation: A Christian Path*, he expressed what is essentially a Western Christian mystical perspective, very much along the lines discussed in this chapter, that is, following the apophatic current that runs from Dionysius the Areopagite through *The Cloud of Unknowing* and directly through to Jäger himself, who after all is founder of the Benediktushaus, a Catholic retreat in Germany. In his earlier books, Zen Buddhism is certainly present at least as background, even if he centers on the Christian line of the Platonic mystical tradition. By the time his books on Christian contemplative life were published in the 1990s, Jäger had long since completed his Zen Buddhist training and was established as a Zen teacher, but he does not foreground that aspect of his inner life.

What makes Jäger so distinctive is that he is deeply versed in both the history and tradition of Christian mysticism and in Zen Buddhism, but what he espouses and teaches is a transconfessional spirituality that he describes explicitly as belonging to the *philosophia perennis*. His embrace of a transconfessional esoteric spirituality is perhaps there already in his books on Christian mysticism, but becomes more visible in *Search for the Meaning of Life*, and is explicit by the time he published *Mysticism for Modern Times*, the transcript of a free-form conversation with Christoph Quarch that is one of the most important works on mysticism published in English in many years.

In Jäger's early books on Christian mysticism, such as *Contemplation: A Christian Path*, he features *The Cloud of Unknowing* and the work of Meister Eckhart, even as he refers frequently to Buddhist traditions and references. Jäger is intimately familiar with the Dionysian-Platonic tradition, offering detailed commentary not only on *The Cloud of Unknowing* but also on its companion treatise, *The Book of Privy Counsel*, one of five works generally attributed to the same anonymous medieval author.[76] Jäger also devotes a section of his book to explicating Eckhart, and here, as in his discussion of *The Cloud of Unknowing*, it is clear that Jäger's analysis is infused with his own direct knowledge of contemplative practice and experience.

Search for the Meaning of Life represents a middle or transitional period in Jäger's work. In it, he reflects on the fact that so many mystics in the Christian tradition were persecuted, imprisoned, or even burned at the stake. And he reflects on the fact that mysticism in the modern period almost vanished from the teachings and practices of Catholicism, let alone from Protestantism, where it was always rare anyway. Here, Jäger muses on the work of oft-condemned "quietist" mystics Madame Guyon and Miguel de Molinos, coming to the conclusion that they were not at all as they were portrayed by their exoteric opponents (that is, proposing mere spiritual passivity) but were actually deeply versed in the object-less contemplative practices that inform the whole of the Platonic mystical tradition within Christianity.[77] Jäger, in this book, begins to come to terms with the fact that the search for ultimate reality is central to what it means to be human and that if seeking individuals do not find support for their esoteric (inner) search within Western religious institutions, then they will "have to set up their tents outside the organized [exoteric] Church because they are rejected inside it."[78]

But it is in his mature books, in particular, *Mysticism for Modern Times* and *West-östliche Weisheit* (*West-Eastern Wisdom*) that Jäger more clearly indicates his East-West synthesis of what he terms a transconfessional spirituality rooted in deep contemplative knowledge and practice. In "Many Paths to One Peak," Jäger remarks that by "transconfessional spirituality" he does not mean a "religion beyond religions," but rather a *religiosity* beyond religions. More and more, he adds, people today are deeply religious without professing faith in a particular religion.[79] He is not endorsing syncretism, he hastens to add, but rather is pointing out that although there are many stained glass windows, behind them is the same light.

Jäger is entirely aware of the tradition of Platonic mysticism and of the Western lineage to which he belongs. Asked about the "jewels of Western mysticism," he responds that the foundation of Western mysticism is Greek. The "whole of Christian mysticism," Jäger continues, is founded in Platonic philosophy. The Neoplatonists, in particular Proclus and Plotinus, were the founders of the *philosophia perennis* carried on "by the great European mystics, such as Meister Eckhart, John of the Cross, Nicholas of Cusa," not to mention "Marguerite Porete, Theresa of Avila, and a figure like Madame Guyon," as well as Jacob Böhme and Angelus Silesius.[80] In brief, Jäger confirms for us once again that Platonism provides the nondual gnostic metaphysics constituting the often-secret architecture of Christian mysticism throughout its long history.[81]

But this Platonic infrastructure of mysticism was never more secret than it is today. When we look at modern literature on mysticism, what we find is that, for all the occasional insights, the vast bulk of it bears very little relationship to the history of Platonic mysticism as we have sketched it here. Today, the word "mysticism" itself is synonymous with "delusion" or "cloudy thinking," and the entire subject is in eclipse, but beyond that, when we look to the scholarship, we find that the majority slights or ignores the vital role that Platonism has for understanding this subject in a coherent way. One could say that Platonic mysticism today has never been more esoteric.

In what follows, we will explore why this is so by surveying the scholarship on mysticism over the past century and a half, and in so doing, draw from it what is most useful, while recognizing that all too often, scholars raise problems the solution to which already is visible in the eclipsed tradition of Platonic mysticism. Contemporary scholarship on mysticism obscures its subject as often as it illuminates it. In our next chapter, we will make our way through much of the literature on mysticism and its role in religion—on the maps scholars have constructed so far—so we can begin to see more clearly where we find ourselves in this largely unexplored continent.

CHAPTER TWO

Mapping Mysticism

It is interesting that, at the beginning of the twentieth century, one finds numerous intellectuals writing about mysticism. It seemed clear to many, more than a century ago, that the exploration of higher states or kinds of consciousness was a central area for scientific, philosophical, and religious research. Major studies were published right at the turn of the century—Richard Bucke's *Cosmic Consciousness* provided a popular context for mysticism, while William James's *Varieties of Religious Experience* and Evelyn Underhill's *Mysticism* sought to provide both general and academic readers with maps for understanding not only discursive but also transcendent dimensions of consciousness. This was a time when it seemed that part of the future of modernity would consist in the exploration of mystical or transcendent dimensions of consciousness. In what follows, we will sketch the modern history of the study of mysticism and, in so doing, see how much work lies ahead if the promise represented by these late nineteenth- and early -twentieth-century explorers and authors still is to be realized.

The study of mysticism began in the nineteenth century, not the late twentieth century. What's more, there was, broadly speaking, a consensus understanding of mysticism during this period. This general understanding has largely been forgotten, however, primarily because it clearly recognizes the central role of Platonism. Once one recognizes that the history of mysticism in Christianity is actually the history of Platonic mysticism in European tradition, then one at once has an essential key. This one insight changes the way one understands mysticism. And this perspective was broadly shared across European, British, and American scholars of mysticism during the period.

Let us take some representative examples. In Eleanor Gregory's *An Introduction to Christian Mysticism* (1901), she begins by remarking, "[W]e fasten on the great name of Plato, who is, it is widely conceded, the father of European Mysticism." She adds, "The name of Plato appears and reappears, in cycles or waves of human thought, all down the centuries," and often is "directly connected with Mysticism."[1] Likewise, for Emily Herman, this was the received understanding of mysticism: "Platonism, Scholasticism, the Renaissance—these were the background of the mystic portrait" and it is "only out of such a background" that "Mysticism can arise."[2] Arguing against a dehistoricized and psychologized understanding of mysticism, Herman presents as classic examples of mysticism combined with metaphysics such luminaries as "Plotinus, Dionysius, Scotus Erigena, Eckhart, and Boehme" and perhaps Aquinas, as well as "the Cambridge Platonists, [Thomas] Traherne, [Samuel Taylor] Coleridge, Wordsworth, and other intellectual contemplatives."[3]

Throughout its history, European mysticism is informed by Platonism. Herman puts it this way: "[T]he great *praparatio mystica* was Platonism, with its commanding intellectual sweep and its noble wonder and reverence."[4] Neoplatonism is "sweet and pure enough to be the main source and inspiration of the finest mediaeval and modern mysticism." Of central importance is "the austere and exalted thought of Plotinus," and in the end, "the main historical source of Mysticism as a reasoned attitude was Alexandrian Platonism."[5] In fact, Herman concludes, what is necessary is "the development of a new Christian Platonism. The only philosophy which can ever yield us a consistent metaphysic of the Christian faith is a new Platonism."[6] Such views are not those of Herman alone; she cites support from other scholars of the time.[7] It is also interesting that, based in a sophisticated understanding of Platonism, scholars of the time often sought to oppose the notion (advanced by William James) of a "double consciousness" at work in mysticism—that is, of mysticism being at odds with reason.[8] Here too the conception is fundamentally Platonic, that intuitive perception of transcendent reality is not separate from, let alone opposed to, reason but rather part of the mind as an integrated whole.

Likewise, another widely influential author on mysticism, Friedrich von Hügel (1852–1925), published a lengthy study of mysticism that focused on St. Catherine of Genoa and her circle. To whom was Catherine obliged most for her mysticism? Von Hügel remarks that Catherine's work "assimilated and further explicated certain Platonic and especially certain Neo-Platonic conceptions." "Her Neo-Platonism," he continues, derived primarily from Dionysius the Areopagite. The exact means of communication, von Hügel writes, between Catherine and her Platonic sources, Plato, Plotinus, and Proclus, is by no means clear, but he is "nevertheless obliged to postulate" its existence.[9] And in an extended discussion, he looks closely at the different aspects of how Plato, Plotinus, Proclus, and Dionysius are visible in the works and thought of Catherine of Genoa.[10]

We also find in the literature of the period the occasional use of the word "esotericism" to describe the tradition of Platonic mysticism. In Edouard Récéjac's *Essay on the Bases of Mysticism*, his model of mysticism is thoroughly Platonic. He writes that "every positive acquisition made in any order of facts whatever, comes from the eternal principles where things are true and good in essence, before manifesting themselves as such in Time."[11] And in this Platonic context, "Science, Art, pure Philosophy, all have their esotericism," but "in the immense region of the things of the soul, how could there be an esotericism more intimate and more reserved than the mystic?"[12] The most important of books are those whose "religious esotericism accords with the best wills and best judgments of all countries and all times," those representing "that *Philosophia perennis*, which, in its various degrees, is the true, sole, and divine Revelation."[13] *Philosophia perennis*, here, refers essentially to Platonic mysticism, and is synonymous with esotericism.

Likewise, Cuthbert Butler in *Western Mysticism: The Teaching of Saints Augustine, Gregory, and Bernard on Contemplation and the Contemplative Life* (1922) seeks to eliminate confusion about the term "mysticism," eliminating "occasional accidental concomitants, as visions, revelations, raptures, or other psycho-physical phenomena," including "telepathy," because these are "psychic, not mystic." The word mysticism, he continues, "should be jealously reserved for its proper traditional religious sense, given it in the beginning by 'Dionysius'—the secret knowledge or perception of God in contemplation."[14] Butler is not all that keen on Neoplatonism as such—he later refers to the Platonic mysticism of Dionysius the Areopagite as "foreign elements" that did not really fit with his own preference for fideistic Christianity—but all the same even he felt it incumbent on him to defer to Dionysius in defining what mysticism is, and is compelled to acknowledge the essential importance of Plotinus in the history of mysticism.[15]

For his part, the Catholic Butler was compelled to acknowledge the vital importance of Plotinus in the history of mysticism because of the emphasis placed upon him by the Anglican priest William Ralph Inge (1860–1954), sometimes referred to as "Dean Inge," since he was Dean of St. Paul's Cathedral. Inge's many books, written in an accessible style, included *Christian Mysticism* (the Bampton Lectures) (1899); *The Religious Philosophy of Plotinus and Some Modern Philosophies of Religion* (1914); *The Philosophy of Plotinus* (the Gifford Lectures) (1918); *The Platonic Tradition in English Religious Thought* (the Hulsean Lectures) (1926), and many others. From the titles alone one can see that Inge emphasized the Platonic nature of mysticism, and indeed, in all of these books Platonism is central to how we are to understand mysticism. In a late book, *Mysticism in Religion* (1947), Inge writes that while the theme of love is emphasized in Christianity, with regard to mysticism "there is not much else that is not at least adumbrated in Plato and Plotinus."[16] Even an author like Arthur Devine, who is disinclined to acknowledge the role of Platonic mysticism, felt compelled to define his terms as set by Dionysius the Areopagite.[17]

Rufus Jones (1863–1948) was a professor of philosophy and psychology at Haverford College, and also an active member of Quakerism, which did influence his writings on mysticism. As later became the norm, he emphasized mystical experience, and inner as opposed to outer forms of religion. Jones does attempt to differentiate Platonic from "New Testament" mysticism, in keeping with his Quakerist Protestantism, but for all that he is compelled to acknowledge that Platonism is the headwaters of all European mysticism.[18] In *Studies in Mystical Religion* (1909), Jones also unambiguously declares that "Platonic philosophy was by far the greatest pre-Christian influence [on mysticism]. In fact it may be said that Plato is the father of *speculative*, as distinguished from simple, implicit, unreflective mysticism."[19] Jones devotes many pages to the explication of Platonism and of how Neoplatonism, chiefly through Plotinus and then Dionysius the Areopagite, came to shape Christian mysticism.[20]

In a book published relatively late in his life, *The Flowering of Mysticism* (1939), Jones reflected on his first exposure to serious scholarship on mysticism, in 1885–1886, when he began to study the work of Karl Schmidt in German and French, and then met Schmidt himself in France. Later Jones came to question Schmidt's account of mysticism, and developed his own mature perspective, writing in *The Flowering of Mysticism* that "The Platonic stream of life and thought is beyond question the greatest single source of European mysticism," and that "Plotinus is in the fullest sense the 'Father' of western mysticism."[21] Above all, Jones continues, Plotinus "explained clearly why that supreme attainment is *beyond thought*. It must transcend the dualism of subject and object in a higher experience of identity. The higher experience for Plotinus is *ecstasy*. With that background of thought he was bound to make the *via negativa* the essential way to the supreme reality."[22] In other words, Jones understood and accurately conveyed the importance of Platonic mysticism in the Western tradition.

By 1920, Edward Ingram Watkin was writing to explicate the tradition of Platonic mysticism against the interpretation of Evelyn Underhill, who wrongly "emphasizes the volitional and sentient aspects of mystical experience at the expense of the cognitive." Watkin tells us explicitly that his purpose is to develop "the metaphysic implicit in mystical experience, a philosophy of mysticism" that "is the body of truth about the nature of ultimate reality and of our relationship to it to be derived from the content of mystical experience."[23] It was then still possible to refer to "ultimate reality" and to a universal metaphysics in the context of the Platonic tradition, even if it was asserted, as Watkin did, against the subjectivism of Underhill, William James, and others. Watkin's Roman Catholicism provided a bulwark against modernism, behind which he could still assert metaphysical objectivity. But this was the period when the metaphysical unity that the Platonic tradition had provided gave way before the centrifugal forces of modernity.

It was fairly common during this period for religious believers to write on the subject of mysticism as religious experience to be understood through mystical theology, and from this confessional perspective, it became sometimes difficult to see why the sublime Plotinus could have written what he did when he was manifestly not Christian. The solution to this problem proposed by Alfred Sharpe, in *Mysticism, Its True Nature and Value* (1910), was that Plotinus represented "one of those manifestations of grace outside its regular channels," "an involuntary witness to the truth of the Christian view of mysticism." But however one seeks to explain it, Sharpe continues, "the fact is that the system of Plotinus, on its mystical side, is practically identical with that of Dionysius and of all Christian mystics."[24] Likewise, Arthur Chandler in *Ara Coeli: An Essay in Mystical Theology* (1909) struggles with the question of how Christian mysticism is to be distinguished from Platonic mysticism, concluding that Plotinian mysticism is "abstract" inasmuch as it is concerned with the One, and Christian mysticism is ultimately about the "Beatific Vision of the Holy Trinity in heaven," and one's relationship with "the Divine Personality."[25] In any case, devoutly Catholic or Anglican books of the period still felt compelled to acknowledge at least something of the Platonic origins of Christian mysticism. However, a new approach to mysticism was developing, one that did not see it in a Platonic Christian context at all, but rather as individual psychological experience. Among those who advanced this new approach was Richard Maurice Bucke.

Richard Maurice Bucke (1837–1902) was trained as a British physician who specialized in psychiatry, later serving as the head of the Asylum for the Insane in Hamilton, Ontario for the last several decades of his life. He was adventurous as a young man, traveling into the wilds of California, helping fight off a war party of Shoshone Indians, losing toes to frostbite, seeking a fortune in silver, but he became most well known not for his adventures, or for his later medical career, so much as for the aftermath of a mystical experience that he had in 1872, while in London. This experience of brief illumination became the centerpoint of his later book, *Cosmic Consciousness*, published in the year before his death.

In *Cosmic Consciousness*, Bucke sought to outline and to contextualize his own mystical experience both in terms of its characteristics, and in terms of the larger history of mysticism. Of these, the most important are the characteristics of mystical experience that he outlined. Bucke, drawing on both his own experiences and on his wide-ranging study of mystics throughout history, concluded that authentic mystical experiences (as opposed to pathologies) 1. tend to take place "suddenly, without warning," "in a flash." It 2. entails a sense of joy or bliss, and 3. entails "intellectual illumination impossible to describe." It reveals the cosmos not as dead matter but as "living presence." And what is more, it demonstrates to one the eternal nature of life, how love is foundational to all existence, and "that the happiness of every individual is in the long run absolutely certain."[26] Hence it entails 4. moral elevation 5. a sense of immortality and freedom from fear of death as well as 6. freedom from a sense that sin exists in the world, and 7. an enduring change in one's being that can be described as a "transfiguration."[27] As a result, Bucke adds, one finds that one has acquired or revealed "enormously greater capacity both for learning and initiating [action]."[28]

Bucke provides a summary of these characteristics for us. They include:

a. The subjective light.

b. The moral elevation.

c. The intellectual illumination.

d. The sense of immortality.

e. The loss of the fear of death.

f. The loss of the sense of sin.

g. The suddenness, instantaneousness, of the awakening.

h. The (importance of the) previous character of the man— intellectual, moral and physical.

i. The age of illumination.

j. The added charm to the personality so that men and women are always (?) strongly attracted to the person.

k. The transfiguration of the subject of the change as seen by others when the cosmic sense is actually present.

Bucke sees these as the characteristics of the next stage of human evolution. Just as one goes through a stage from animal to human self-awareness, being aware of oneself in relation to an external world, so too one can go through a stage from human self-awareness to what Bucke calls "cosmic consciousness," or mystical illumination.

Bucke also gives a whole series of exemplary figures, beginning with Buddha and Jesus, and including Plotinus, Dante, St. John of the Cross, Francis Bacon, Jacob Böhme, William Blake, Walt Whitman, and Edward Carpenter. With them, Bucke seeks to substantiate his posited general characteristics of mystical experiences, using copious quotations from various texts, Buddhist, Christian, Neoplatonic, and literary (as in the cases of Dante, Blake, and Whitman). One of the most interesting of Bucke's exemplary figures, though, is Edward Carpenter, who was a contemporary of Bucke's and like Bucke, an avid reader of Whitman and an author (a poet and essayist) in his own right. Carpenter exchanged correspondence with Bucke about his mystical experiences, and wrote at one point about his illumination that

> I really do not feel that I can tell you anything without falsifying and obscuring the matter. I have done my best to write it out in *Towards Democracy*. I have no experience of physical light in this relation. The perception seems to be one in which all the senses unite into one sense. In which *you become* the object. But this is unintelligible, mentally speaking. I do not think the matter can be defined as yet; but I do not know that there is any harm in writing about it.[29]

One might point out Carpenter's remark that "*you become* the object," which is significant because it expresses in contemporary language of subject and object what would have been expressed in more symbolic or gnomic language in an earlier era.

From Carpenter's example, Bucke then extracts again a series of concluding points as a summary. In Carpenter's case, he writes,

a. Illumination occurred at the characteristic age—in the thirty-seventh year.

b. And in the characteristic season—in the spring.

c. There was a sense of "inward light," but not strictly the usual experience of subjective light.

d. There was the usual sudden intellectual illumination,

e. And the usual sudden moral elevation.

f. His life was absolutely governed henceforth by the new light that had dawned upon him—"it held his feet."

g. He lost, absolutely, upon illumination, the sense of sin.

h. He clearly saw himself to be immortal.

i. But the best proof of Cosmic Consciousness in his case is his description thereof, which could only be drawn (as he tells us it was) from his own experience.[30]

What makes Bucke particularly valuable is this inclination to extract general characteristics, to generalize, to seek to understand not only the particular case, but also to see what broader conclusions can be drawn from it.

William James's (1842–1910) approach to mysticism was actually quite similar to that of Bucke. After all, they both were trained in medicine. James, however, never practiced medicine, but instead became a professor at Harvard University, first of physiology, then of philosophy. It is perhaps significant, given our earlier survey of Platonic mysticism, that William James's godfather was Ralph Waldo Emerson. Unlike Emerson, James did not seem to have (or at least, professed not to have had) any mystical experiences of his own, but nonetheless he can be understood to be in the American intellectual lineage of Emerson and to have brought to this lineage a scientific approach, that is, an effort like Bucke's to survey, characterize, and understand the phenomenon of mysticism.

James's approach to religion in general is rather different from scholarly tendencies in the century after him. Whereas the academic study of religion, as it developed in the last half of the twentieth century and the first quarter of the twenty-first century, tended toward an emphasis on institutional religion, sociological approaches, and eventually "material culture" (which has the advantage of allowing one to avoid pesky ideas, let alone metaphysics), James emphasized the role of what he termed "religious genius," often founding figures, from whom the social institutions later sometimes developed. James also emphasized the role of religious experience, which he urged scholars to consider and analyze.

An overview of *Varieties of Religious Experience*, James's Gifford Lectures in 1901–1902, is in order. James begins by making clear that he writes as a psychologist, interested primarily in the psychology of the religious individual, and not in social or institutional phenomena.[31] His first chapter is called "Religion and Neurology," and subsequent chapters include "The Religion of Healthy-Mindedness," "The Sick Soul," and "The Divided Self, and the Process of Its Unification." In other words, the clear focus of James's book is on religion and the psychology of the individual personality. It is not until lectures (chapters) 16 and 17 that James comes to the subject of mysticism itself.

James has in mind an empirical approach to mysticism, seen as a general phenomenon he regards as central to religious experience regardless of the particular tradition. He believes that "personal religious experience has its root and centre in mystical states of consciousness."[32] In order to avoid the vague uses to which the word "mysticism" is subject, James seeks to define its characteristics. These are

1. *Ineffability*: "it defies expression," "no adequate report of its contents can be given in words," and "it must be directly experienced; it cannot be imparted or transferred to others." Thus, "mystical states are more like states of feeling than like states of intellect."

2. *Noetic quality*: mystical states are "states of insight into depths of truth unplumbed by the discursive intellect"; they are "illuminations, revelations," and "all inarticulate though they remain."

3. *Transiency*: "Mystical states cannot be sustained for long. Except in rare instances, half an hour or at most an hour or two, seems to be the limit beyond which they fade into the light of common day."

4. *Passivity*: although the states may be brought about by practices like "fixing the attention, . . . the mystic feels as if his own will were in abeyance, and indeed sometimes as if he were grasped and held by a superior power."[33]

Strikingly, James's immediately subsequent text does not include examples from figures generally recognized as classically mystical, for instance, Dionysius the Areopagite, Meister Eckhart, or others in the accepted tradition of Western European Christian mysticism, but rather adduces examples from literature and from the newly developing science of anesthetics. When one has spent considerable time with the body of literature on mysticism that predates and is contemporary with James, one cannot help but be struck by the disconnection of James's explication of mysticism from the larger context of contemporary scholarship.

In fact, James begins his explication of mysticism after listing his four characteristics not with mystics, but with a hodgepodge of literary references to "certain poems" that can serve as "irrational doorways" through which "the wildness and the pang of life, stole into our hearts and thrilled them."[34] He refers to the feeling of déjà vu, to "dreamy states" of consciousness, to "trance," and to the poet

John Addington Symonds's vague sense when in church or reading or somewhere a "mood" that "disappeared in a series of rapid sensations which resembled the awakening from anaesthetic influence." This, he said, was a "kind of trance" that Symonds "disliked" because "I cannot even now find words to render it intelligible," though it consisted in his awareness of only a "pure, absolute, abstract Self" accompanied by a "grim conviction" that he had arrived at a demonstration of "eternal Maya or illusion."[35] James then goes on to discuss his experience under nitrous oxide sedation, as well as friends who "believe in the anaesthetic revelation," that is, in the sedation by nitrous oxide producing "mystical consciousness."[36] And James adduces the example again of J. A. Symonds, in this case because he claimed a kind of ecstatic experience followed upon the administration of chloroform.[37]

It is only after citing a few more literary figures, including Walt Whitman, then drawing on the book *Cosmic Consciousness* by R. M. Bucke, then looking at Vedanta, Buddhism, and Sufism with particular attention to the ascent of consciousness through absorption or concentration, and then looking at the works of St. John of the Cross and Theresa of Avila, that James finally gets to the essential current of Platonic mysticism as represented by Dionysius the Areopagite and Plotinus, as well as Eckhart, and Angelus Silesius.[38] But get there he does, and he concludes with three main points about mystical experiences:

1. Mystical states "when well developed, usually are, and have the right to be, absolutely authoritative over the individuals to whom they come."

2. "No authority emanates from them which should make it a duty for those who stand outside of them to accept their revelations uncritically."

3. "They break down the authority of the non-mystical or rationalistic consciousness," showing it "to be only one kind of consciousness," and "open out the possibility of other orders of truth."[39] A mystic is one who has been "there," and who knows it. "It is vain for rationalism to grumble about this."[40]

What James offers is an empirical approach to mysticism, one that acknowledges that some states of consciousness alleged to be mystical may in fact be states of psychological disorder, but that nonetheless one cannot rule out the possibility that there are indeed higher states of consciousness toward which mystical literature points, and that in fact these may be "indispensable stages in our approach to the final fullness of the truth."[41] Furthermore, he expresses considerable doubt about the utility of rationalistic theology and discursive religious philosophy, which he regards as "secondary products," while "feeling is the deeper source of religion."[42] And he then comes to one of his most important points, which is to endorse a "critical Science of Religions" that ultimately may approach something like a science of optics in its precision, verified by those who can see, and accepted by the blind as having veracity.[43]

Thus James provides the basis for what B. Alan Wallace terms in the early twenty-first century a contemplative science, an empirical approach to consciousness with a scientific foundation that includes neuroscience and other fields but incorporates the direct experiences and verifications of contemplative practitioners such as Wallace, a Buddhist teacher of meditation as well as an academic author.[44] Wallace has expressed great admiration for James and regards him as a vitally important figure for the study of consciousness. James did open out the study of mysticism into a cross-cultural and pan-religious approach, but in doing so he also diminished the central role of Platonic mysticism in understanding European mysticism.

Following upon the works of Bucke and James, Evelyn Underhill's sprawling work on mysticism, and in particular her widely disseminated book *Mysticism* (1911), which went through numerous expansions, contributed to the subsequent almost total eclipse of Platonic mysticism. Although her bibliography and text make clear she was aware of the tradition of Platonic mysticism, she had an ambivalent response to it. Early in *Mysticism*, she quotes Plato in the *Timaeus*, who asks, "What is that which Is and has no Becoming, and what is that which is always becoming and never Is?" Underhill's comment is that "without necessarily subscribing to the Platonic answer to this question," "the question itself is sound and worth asking."[45] Underhill seeks to differentiate her understanding of Christian mysticism from Platonic mysticism.

Early in *Mysticism*, she addresses Platonic mysticism directly. Her view of it is that Platonism is intellectual and theoretical; it is, she thinks, "the reaction of the intellectualist upon mystical truth."[46] "We could not well dispense with our Christian Platonists and mystical philosophers. They are our stepping-stones to higher things,"

Underhill writes, asserting furthermore, "They are no more mystics than the milestones on the Dover Road are travelers to Calais."[47] Sometimes, she admits, "their words—the wistful words of those who know but cannot be—produce mystics." But she is convinced that Platonic mysticism is not authentic mysticism.

In part, Underhill's conviction is a result of the time in which she lived. She represents an influential and transitional figure. By the time *Mysticism* was first published—let alone its later editions—William James's *Varieties of Religious Experience* had long been available. Richard Bucke's *Cosmic Consciousness* also had been available for some years. Both books have in common several aspects that we find also in Underhill. First, all three point toward mysticism as individual religious experience, in James's and Bucke's case, even irrespective of cultural or religious context. Second, all three list what they see as characteristics of individual mystical experience. Third, all three, but particularly James and Underhill, help inaugurate what we may term the psychologization of mysticism.

Underhill wrote in the context of having read all of the authors we've discussed so far, and she recognized that the most influential of them was William James. She takes some time to get to his discussion of mysticism, spending many pages meandering through divagations on the theme, defining mysticism in passing as "non-individualistic," as "the abolition of individuality," as "a movement of the heart, seeking to transcend the limitations of the individual standpoint," "purely from an instinct of love."[48] And she writes that "true and first-hand mystical experience" presents the hallmark of "imparting to the reader a sense of exalted and extended life."[49] To this she adds, "[W]e have already reached a point at which William James's celebrated 'four marks' of the mystic state, Ineffability, Noetic Quality, Transiency and Passivity will fail to satisfy us." In their place, she offers four tests for mysticism of her own:

1. "True mysticism is active and practical, not passive and theoretical . . . something which the whole self does."

2. "Its aims are wholly transcendental and spiritual," having nothing to do with exploring, improving, or changing the cosmos.

3. The mystic seeks "not merely the Reality of all that is," but also "a living and personal Object of Love" under "the guidance of the heart."

4. "Living union with this One. . . . is a definite state or form of enhanced life." It is neither intellectual alone nor emotional alone, but is arrived at by a "psychological and spiritual process" that results in "the liberation of a new, or rather latent, form of consciousness," "ecstasy," and "the Unitive State."[50]

Underhill differs to some extent with James, but nonetheless recognizes truth in what he says. Essentially, Underhill wants to emphasize that mysticism is an inner process that engages the heart as well as the intellect, and that it is both psychological and spiritual. Thus, for her, James's notion that an anesthetic could generate mysticism is not valid; mysticism is not just anything. At the same time, she acknowledges that "ineffability" and "noetic quality" are indeed characteristics of "contemplative experience."[51] A poet might have a glimpse of transcendence, but "Contemplation" is "positive attainment of the Absolute" in a "*whole act.*" Contemplation, she continues, entails "an experience of the All" that "is *given* rather than attained," and that "is apprehended by way of participation, not by way of observation." These she terms "The Totality and the Givenness of the Object" and "Self-Mergence of the subject."[52] In short, "God is self-disclosed to the soul," and "the soul rushes out willingly to lose itself in Him." Thus a "divine osmosis" is "set up between the finite and the Infinite life."[53]

Likewise, she acknowledges but also takes issue with Bucke. She recognizes that there is a state of "the awakening of the mystical consciousness in respect of the World of Becoming," an awareness of everything in nature as renewed and glorious, something extolled in the poetry of Walt Whitman, which Bucke "labeled and described as "Cosmic Consciousness."[54] However, this sense of union with the natural world is "not the final object of the mystic's journey, but it is "one-half" of it; it is but a glimpse through "the heavenly door" for one who has not escaped from "the bonds of his selfhood." It is a recognition that the divine is visible in the world of becoming, "the apprehension of a splendor without," a vision of a transfigured world, but it is not yet transcendence of self and realization of the life within.[55]

Underhill is a transitional figure, important for many reasons. Her work is so sprawling and prolix, so much a palimpsest of quotations and observations one atop another that it is impossible to summarize and for many people, to get through. Her book on mysticism, important as it is and her magnum opus, is one of those books that everyone owns and almost no one has read all the way through. Clearly, she had read and had developed opinions on virtually every mystic and everything written about mysticism during and up to her time. And like virtually every other scholar, she both rejects and absorbs what they have to say. As a result, she is a conduit for the tradition of Platonic mysticism that she also critiques and to which she does not fully belong.

Thus, in a later book intended for a popular audience, *Practical Mysticism*, Underhill defines mysticism as "the art of union with Reality. The mystic is a person who has attained that union in greater or less[er] degree; or who aims at and believes in such attainment."[56] The term "Reality" with a capital R vaguely alludes to Platonic metaphysics; she refers also to "pure Intellect," to "Ultimate Beauty," and to "the Transcendent," all of which show that behind her depiction of mysticism is a Platonic worldview.[57] At the same time, she associates Platonism with intellectualism in the modern sense and insists on the importance of love and of faith in a theistic tradition. For all her passing slights of Platonism, her work could not exist were it not for Platonic mysticism. Virtually all of her metaphysics comes from the Platonic tradition, but without explicitly referring to it.

Hence Underhill is also antecedent to subsequent treatments of mysticism in which Platonic mysticism does not seem to exist at all. There are a number of reasons for this eclipse, among them the decline of attention in philosophy and religion to the role of Neoplatonism in Western European tradition. (Today the vast majority of undergraduates I encounter have never heard of Plato or Platonism, have never read the dialogues, and even those who have, never have heard of Plotinus, let alone Dionysius the Areopagite.) This corresponds to many scholarly approaches to mysticism in the late twentieth and early twenty-first centuries where again Platonic mysticism (contrary to the importance it had in late -nineteenth-century scholarship) did not really exist or seem to have a bearing on the subject "mysticism."

One way that Underhill contributed a little to this eclipse is bound up with an intrinsic tension in Christianity between its confessional, doctrinal traditions and its mystical traditions. Underhill never fully resolved this tension. In Platonic mysticism, the highest gnosis is expressed in terms of negations, and those negations do not leave

room for the continuation of a division between the individual soul
and God. The negations of Dionysius the Areopagite's *Mystical Theology* correspond to the transcendent negations of the Platonic tradition
more broadly, in which as the individual consciousness begins to
recognize its own true nature, it recognizes it as ultimately the same
as the true nature beyond being. In confessional Christian doctrine,
however, the transcendence of subject and object (soul and God) is
borderline heretical; confessional Christianity often wants to maintain
the distinction between soul and God. Underhill clearly is on the side
of mysticism in this tension, but she nonetheless also conveys some
of confessional Christianity in her voluminous writings, and she is
quite well aware of the tension between the two.[58]

Underhill is a transitional figure, then, in the following ways.
Before her, James, and Bucke, mysticism was understood chiefly in
terms of the tradition of Platonic mysticism, represented par excellence by Dionysius the Areopagite and those who belong to the tradition he brought into being in the Christian world. After Underhill,
James, and Bucke, the term "mysticism" took on a fundamentally
different group of associations. Those associations are as follows.

1. Mysticism becomes psychological and individualized. The
    term "mystical experience" becomes an important marker
    of this change.

2. Mysticism is characterized by typologies; it becomes a
    category of psychological experience that is held to have
    identifier marks.

3. Mysticism is cross-cultural; the term "mysticism"
    becomes elastic and can be applied not only to the three
    monotheistic traditions of Christianity, Judaism, and
    Islam, but also to Buddhism and Hinduism, and in some
    cases to indigenous religious traditions in the Americas
    or elsewhere, perhaps even to all religious traditions in
    principle.

4. The specificity and continuity of Platonic mysticism in
    Christianity is not seen as particularly important.

All of these become hallmarks of most subsequent scholarship
on mysticism, by comparison to which Underhill's work is relatively

deeply imbued with the tradition of Platonic mysticism. She refers to it frequently, and without doubt it informs her perspective throughout. By contrast, when, nearly a century later, there were various debates between those who championed mysticism as an "innate human capacity" and those who argued that mysticism was fundamentally a linguistic-social-cultural construct, those debates took place on the terms above. That is, in the terrain represented by the term "mysticism" in such debates, Platonic mysticism was largely a parenthetical inclusion in an argument that typically emphasized Hinduism (for those favoring mysticism as "innate capacity") and Judaism (for those favoring mysticism as a construct), but it was in both cases transcultural in its claims.[59] And it existed in a context shaped by William James's emphasis on psychology, to such an extent that Forman champions a model he terms "perennial psychology" as the best way to understand mysticism.[60]

All of the prevailing tendencies in later scholarship on mysticism have two primary consequences. The first is that the central importance of Platonic mysticism becomes largely overlooked in favor of pan-traditional approaches centered on individual psychological experiences. This is ironic, of course, because Platonism in fact offers a metaphysical and cosmological framework within which one can place and understand mysticism (and individual mystical experiences). But Platonism and Platonic mysticism are fatally inconvenient for the modern project precisely *because* of Platonic metaphysics. This is the second consequence: the importance of Platonic metaphysics is eclipsed.

In our next chapter, we'll chart that eclipse and its effects.

CHAPTER THREE

The Eclipse of Platonic Mysticism

We have seen that there was, broadly speaking, a consensus in late nineteenth-century scholarship about the origin and nature of mysticism as fundamentally Platonic. And we saw how three influential scholars both recognized and conveyed this insight, but also had the effect of inaugurating what became the occultation of Platonic mysticism. This occultation came about primarily because of the modern inclination to view mysticism largely as a spontaneous individual phenomenon without reference to the historical lineage of Platonism conveyed within Christianity through mysticism, and without the historical context of Platonism, the term "mysticism" eventually could be said to mean almost anything.

There are a few mystics whose work we should mention here because they also exemplify this tendency I am calling the eclipse of Platonism. The first is Franklin Merrell-Wolff (1887–1985), author of a number of books detailing an enduring change in consciousness that he termed "without an object."[1] Merrell-Wolff's works detail the implications of change in consciousness, which he describes largely in relation to Vedanta and Buddhism.

Franklin Fowler Wolff, so christened in Pasadena, California, in 1887, was raised as a Methodist, but in adolescence he left Christianity behind. He went to Stanford, where he studied mathematics and philosophy, and later studied at Harvard. In 1914, he returned to Stanford, where he taught mathematics, but in 1915, he left academia. He lived in the San Fernando Valley. In 1920, he married Sarah Merrell Briggs, and they chose to take one another's names—

hence he became Franklin Merrell-Wolff. He and his wife, later named Sherifa Merrell-Wolff, founded an esoteric group called the Assembly of Man in 1928, and built an ashram in the Sierra Nevada mountains near Mount Whitney, the highest point in the contiguous United States.[2] Sherifa died in 1959, and Merrell-Wolff remarried, living in a house in the mountains until his death at ninety-eight in 1985. He had a number of students and followers, and he left behind various books on his mystical experiences and philosophy, as well as a large library of audio recordings of his thought.

Merrell-Wolff's publications and recordings represent a life's work centered on his spiritual realizations—it is a consistent and extensive body of work with a unique vocabulary and set of concepts. It is also unusual because, although it was certainly possible for Merrell-Wolff to have created a religion, or a religious tradition to come after him, he consciously refrained from doing or encouraging this. Rather, he simply detailed the nature of his mystical realizations and their implications and the ways that they corresponded to Vedanta, Buddhism, and other religious and philosophical traditions. Ron Leonard—who wrote his doctoral dissertation and a subsequent monograph on this subject—unambiguously remarks, "Wolff's philosophy owes nothing essential to any external authority."[3] Of course, one has to doubt this, based on Merrell-Wolff's own account.

Merrell-Wolff recounts his experiences in *Pathways Through to Space*, recalling "some years now have passed since the precipitation of the inner events that led to the writing of this book."[4] *Pathways Through to Space* provides a fascinating account of his mystical experiences in the summer of 1936, which he calls the beginning of his "ineffable transition." He does describe elsewhere how he spent years, beginning with his time at Harvard, studying the ancient Greeks, as well as Buddhism and Hinduism. And what he calls his "Fundamental Realization" does not appear to have been occasioned by meditation practice as generally understood; he says that practices differ between occidental and oriental cultures.[5]

In the mountains of California, on a gold-mining expedition, Merrell-Wolff experienced what he called the "Current of Ambrosia." He was "above space, time, and causality," having no interest in worldly pursuits, in a state of bliss, with only "the desire that other souls should also realize this that I had realized, for in it lay the one effective key for the solving of their problems."[6] Others in his presence also experienced the Current, and he found he also could induce it in or conduct it to others if they were capable of recognizing it. He induced it in himself simply by turning his attention to it. What he called his "Fundamental Realization" led to a state of "High Indifference," that is, of transcendent consciousness without an object. His written work elaborates the significances of these mystical experiences.

At the heart of Merrell-Wolff's mystical account is the realization of "Primordial Consciousness," which "transcended both subject and object, but was, in itself, entirely unaffected by the presence or absence of either." "This Primordial Consciousness . . . is the common ontological ground of all forms of consciousness, regardless of content," which Merrell-Wolff also terms "consciousness without an object or subject," as well as "Great Space" and "Light."[7] Merrell-Wolff explains: "Primordial Consciousness cannot be described as conceptual, affective, or perceptual." He goes on to say, "It is a deep, substantial, and vital sort of consciousness," one that does not belong to a field of relationships and that is ontologically prior to the existence or absence of objects or subjects; it is more akin to a metaontological continuum and can only be recognized through consciousness becoming aware of itself.[8]

Now all of this would appear to have little to do with Platonic mysticism, but in fact when one delves deeply enough into Merrell-Wolff's work, one finds that behind the scenes, as it were, he belongs to that tradition. Of course he was influenced by Shankaracarya and Vedanta, as well as by Buddhism—but in his book on metaphysics, Merrell-Wolff, a mathematician by training, recalled how during his studies at Harvard, he familiarized himself with the Pythagorean and Platonic traditions. Early on, he said, he realized that "a considerable portion of western philosophy from the Greeks to the present day seemed to imply some sort of insight into Reality that was not reducible to observation."[9] Elsewhere, after a discussion of Plato, Merrell-Wolff concludes that there is a kind of knowledge he calls "Knowledge through Identity" "that is neither conceptual nor perceptual and consequently can neither be defined in the strict sense of the word nor be experienced." But through awakening, one can recognize oneself as "identical with It."[10] In other words, Merrell-Wolff had come to a perspective regarding Platonic mysticism akin to what has been expressed in this book.

In another book, this one dedicated largely to metaphysics, Merrell-Wolff incisively analyzes "pragmatism," by which he means chiefly but not exclusively scientific materialism, as "anti-intellectual" and "prosensational," as well as "anti-transcendental," meaning that its adherents believe that "sensational experience" is more "bedded in the Real" than the intellect, and they deny the reality of any gnostic or "supramental" knowledge. He then goes on to analyze "Transcendentalism" which he defines not as a product of reason or speculation (though it could be) but ideally of gnostic realization.[11] And he quotes at length from Plotinus's letter to Flaccus, which had been reprinted both by Richard Bucke in *Cosmic Consciousness* and by Ralph Vaughn in *Hours with the Mystics*, and which emphasizes knowledge of inner identity that transcends subject and object, termed "illumination."[12]

In other words, when one looks for it in Merrell-Wolff's work, one definitely can see that he was well aware of and influenced by the Platonic tradition, and particularly by Plotinus. Of course he was primarily drawing on his own direct experience and explicating it and its significances, but he does so in the larger context of Vedanta, Buddhism, and Platonic mysticism. At the same time, one has to *look* for the third of these; for the general reader, Platonic mysticism is largely invisible in Merrell-Wolff's work, present only in a few direct allusions or for those who can recognize it in what and how he is describing what he terms mystical or gnostic realization and its implications.

We would be remiss if we didn't include Aldous Huxley's influential *The Perennial Philosophy* (1944) here. Huxley was, of course, a popular writer rather than a scholar of mysticism, but he did include in this collection copious selections from Eckhart, Ruysbroek, and even a few selections from Cambridge Platonists John Smith and Benjamin Whichcote, as well as from *The Cloud of Unknowing*.[13] But these are scattered higgledy-piggledy among all manner of other religious and literary figures and quotations. It is an important collection and made the term "perennial philosophy" widely known, but at the same time it effectively obscured the prior understanding both of Platonic mysticism and of perennial philosophy in favor of what we might call a wild comparativism. That is, the theistic St. Bernard of Clairvaux is juxtaposed with the *Tao te ching*, which is next to William Law, not far from the poet Rumi or from Boethius. As a result, Huxley's book inaugurated what later became the eclipse, by wide-ranging comparativism, of Platonic mysticism and of perennial philosophy.

But there were works whose authors recognized Platonic mysticism and emphasized it. Such was the perspective expressed by Walter

Terence Stace in *Mysticism and Philosophy*, a decade and a half after Huxley's book was first published. Stace, who had just retired as professor of philosophy at Princeton, dared to venture into the forbidden territory of mysticism, and the conclusions he came to were on the whole quite close to our own. He did attempt to differentiate between what he termed "extrovertive" mysticism (a virtually identical mysticism that includes a transsubjective recognition of identity with the cosmos, or what Richard Maurice Bucke called "cosmic consciousness"); and "introvertive" mysticism, which is his term for traditional contemplative ascent and realization. However, one has to wonder whether this is a distinction without a fundamental difference, since unitive consciousness as described by negative theology does not lend itself to such a division into categories. Indeed, even Stace himself laid relatively little emphasis on it, and the two categories only differed, if at all, on one minor aspect.[14]

Much more important were Stace's conclusions at the end of his seminal book, especially on the subject of "Mysticism and Religion." There, he concludes that mysticism as he discusses it in his book (primarily with regard to negative theology and examples like Meister Eckhart) is not necessarily religious. Of this mysticism without religion, he offers Plotinus as a key exemplar, and what is more, he recognizes that mysticism as it emerged in Christianity owed much to Greece and to Platonism, comparatively little to Judaism. In recognizing the individualized nature of mysticism, Stace concludes that mystical consciousness does not require any particular organized religion and that it is possible to throw off a creed and still be a mystic. For Stace, mystical experiences have seven characteristics (incorporating some of the four of William James): unity, ineffability, noetic quality, "a feeling of blessedness," "awareness of the holy, sacred, or divine," paradoxicality, and transsubjectivity. The last two express what I have been terming the transcendence of subject and object, paradoxicality meaning an experience might be fullness but emptiness, full of content but contentless, transsubjectivity meaning that the experience is nondual or beyond individual identity. Stace is an important figure because his analysis of mysticism corresponds quite well with and clearly reflects the tradition of Platonic mysticism.

It is true that Stace draws on a wide range of sources and traditions in order to make his case, but his criteria and his typology are based in the *via negativa* tradition of Platonic mysticism. Even his descriptions of "introvertive" and "extrovertive" mysticism are exactly the same, with the minor exception that perhaps "extrovertive mysticism" rather than being "non-spatial and non-temporal" is linked to "an inner subjectivity, or life, in all things."[15] In other words, fundamentally, there is virtually no difference between these two categories, which are more like inflections of the same phenomenon. But most interesting of all, Stace forthrightly recognizes, near the end of his study, that what he is characterizing as mysticism actually is nontheistic at core, that "the essence of the introvertive experience is the undifferentiated unity." There is, he thinks, no convincing evidence that Jesus himself was a mystic (whereas Gautama Buddha was), and this helps explain why mysticism (defined in terms of Platonic mysticism) is only carried along as a current in monotheistic traditions.[16] In other words, Stace's conclusions confirm the argument put forward in this book.

While he was not a specialist in mysticism as such, Mircea Eliade also is important because at the center of his work is a Platonic model. Eliade recognizes the centrality of transcendence for understanding religion, whether shamanic and "primitive" or otherwise: he makes clear that the symbolism of ascent and flight represents the human aspiration to go "above" the human condition; and the axis or Pole symbolizes a return to primordiality prior to time or history, a return to timelessness or eternity. Contemplative ascent and transcendence are central of Eliade's many comparative writings on religion.[17] These concepts reflect Eliade's underlying Platonism and are shaped also by his study and understanding of Indian yoga and Vedanta especially. But Eliade's Platonism is so highly simplified and abstracted as to only be comprehensible as Platonic if this is directly pointed out; Eliade's Platonism is implicit.

The same period—the 1960s and 1970s—gave way to more and more comparativist models. Some of those were overtly anti-mystical, as was for example Robert Charles Zaehner's confusion of mysticism and psychosis. In *Our Savage God: The Perverse Use of Eastern Thought* (1974), for instance, Zaehner claims that a *kensho* or enlightenment experience in Zen Buddhism is with "absolutely no doubt at all" "precisely and exactly" the mystical experience of Charles Manson (!). Zaehner actually goes on to speculate that someone who experienced a Zen Buddhist awakening would thereafter be "vicariously murdering the 'innocent' citizens of Tokyo." It is particularly interesting that Zaehner attacks those who espouse perennial philosophy as failing to recognize distinctions between religious traditions—when in his conflation of Manson and Zen Buddhism, he spectacularly fails to recognize obvious distinctions between religious traditions and between religions and psychosis.[18] What Zaehner thinks of as "mysticism" he associates with the use of hallucinogens like mescaline, and with Aldous Huxley's perennial philosophy, that is, with a pastiche of different religious traditions. It is extremely difficult to take Zaehner even remotely seriously, so bizarre is his treatment of the subject. And not surprisingly, Plato, Platonism, and Plotinus rate hardly a mention in his work. The term "mysticism" here has become a floating signifier.

The same is true of numerous subsequent authors on mysticism from the 1960s and 1970s on: the more "mysticism" became a comparative category defined as cutting across multiple religious traditions, the less specific meaning it necessarily has. Thus, for instance, Frits Staal, in his *Exploring Mysticism: A Methodological Essay* (1975); William Wainwright, in *Mysticism: A Study of Its Nature, Cognitive Value, and Moral Implications* (1981); Leonard Angel, in *Enlightenment East and West* (1994); Robert Ellwood, in *Mysticism and Religion* (1999); and Randall Studstill, in *The Unity of Mystical Traditions: The Transformation of Consciousness in Tibetan and German Mysticism* (2005), all seek to clarify what mysticism is in a comparative context. Throughout, because of the efforts to understand "mysticism" as a term that fits numerous different religious traditions and phenomena, these scholars are compelled to create schemas that are broad enough to fit numerous and diverse religious traditions, and that as a result relegate Platonic mysticism to the far background.

Robert Ellwood, for instance, defines mysticism by saying that "mystical experience is experience in a religious context that is immediately or subsequently *interpreted* by the experiencer as a direct, unmediated encounter with ultimate divine reality." This definition is crafted to include many religious traditions, for instance, Christian, Muslim, and Hindu, and also including "experiences of divine or transcendent or superhuman beings or states of reality."[19] This is a reasonable working definition if the scope of mysticism is across multiple religious traditions and also includes visionary encounters with divine or transcendent beings. But precisely because it encompasses so much comparativist territory, definitions like this bear an only tangential or distant relationship to Platonic mysticism.

Steven Katz's "constructivist" critique of mysticism also belongs in a comparativist context.[20] Katz, whose primary work is in the study of Judaism and in activism for Israel, argued that mystical experience is filtered through (or "constructed by") language and culture, which is of course true in some respects, but as an argument, nonetheless does not gainsay the possibility of contemplative ascent and transcendence as it appears in the Platonic tradition. Some, taking Katz's critique even further, claimed that mysticism is ultimately a product of *only* language and culture; that there is no such thing as mystical experience in itself, that is, pure mystical transcendence.[21] But simply asserting that there is no such possibility does not make the possibility vanish, however vociferous one's assertion might be.

Comparativism is central to the eclipse of Platonic mysticism, and we see this exemplified also in the work of Katz, in a collection he edited called *Comparative Mysticism: An Anthology of Original Sources* (2013). In this collection, the largest and first part is given to Jewish mysticism, about 150 pages. About 90 pages are devoted to Christian mysticism, and several of those pages, in the middle of the selection, are devoted to Dionysius the Areopagite and Meister Eckhart. There are lengthy sections of Hindu and Buddhist as well as Native American texts, and as might be expected, Katz in his introduction emphasizes that the mystical "experience" "is shaped by concepts which the mystic brings to, and which shape, his or her experience."[22] Thus "the Christian does not experience some unidentified reality, which he or she then conveniently labels 'God,' but rather has at least partially prefigured Christian conceptions of God, or Jesus, or the like." In Katz's view, "the Christian pre-mystical consciousness informs the mystical consciousness" so that the mystic experiences "the mystic reality in terms of Jesus, the Trinity, or a personal God rather than in terms of the nonpersonal, noneverything Buddhist doctrine of *nirvana*."[23]

By beginning with and emphasizing Jewish theistic mysticism, as well as the theistic aspects of Christianity, Katz's collection taken as a whole represents an almost total eclipse of the tradition of Platonic mysticism in favor of a comparativism designed to underscore the differences between heterogenous religions and thus to support his theory of constructivism. In turn, however, this raises the intrinsic conflict between Platonic mysticism—which is "trans-subjective," or nondualistic—and a monotheistic religion that emphasizes separation between a deity and a worshipper. This separation is actually acute, perhaps even most acute, in a tradition of worshipping a tribal god that emphasizes one's own people as the elect or chosen and others as lesser or as lost. Indeed, a Jewish scholar has argued strongly that one shouldn't even use the term "Jewish mysticism."[24] There is an intrinsic and often unresolved contradiction between Platonic mysticism and any theistic tradition in which it finds itself.

W. T. Stace alluded to this issue when he noted that mysticism is "only a minor strand in Christianity, Islam, and Judaism."[25] It is so because monotheistic religions tend to be very uneasy about mystical traditions of subject-object transcendence, which belong in the end to "Greece," "not" "Palestine."[26] Hence Dionysius says of the divine reality that "it belongs neither to the category of existence, nor to that of non-existence."[27] Stace comments that strictly speaking, a theist should recognize that ultimate reality cannot be understood as "objective," because it "transcends altogether the common distinction between subjective and objective."[28] But to do so is to threaten the doctrinal, social, cultural, tribal, or other power systems that are intrinsically based in the dualism of a subject worshipper and an objective deity that in turn creates a whole category of those who seek to mediate between the two.

Robert K. C. Forman, a scholar of religion and practitioner of the new religion Transcendental Meditation (TM), argued against Katz and in favor of what he termed a "dualistic mystical state (DMS)."[29] A "dualistic mystical state" means that while one experiences events in the phenomenal world, one also has an enduring separate "witness" aspect of consciousness. This "witness" aspect of consciousness Forman says he experienced as a result of TM, and he terms it "enlightenment."[30] This "witness" consciousness is akin to the *atman* in Hinduism. Forman also emphasizes what he terms a "Pure Consciousness Event" (PCE) as the heart of mysticism, and the PCE is a category meant to cut across many religious traditions. Whether we can describe the mystical theology of Dionysius the Areopagite or *The Cloud of Unknowing* as reflecting a "dualistic mystical state" or a "pure consciousness event" seems to me highly doubtful, however, because whereas these terms emphasize particular states of reflective consciousness or events in consciousness, apophatic mystical treatises refer not to doubled consciousness or to particular mental events, but to the transcendence of all conceptual or sensory referents.

What's most interesting to me about the 1990s debate between Forman and Katz is that both sides manage to sidestep what I am terming Platonic mysticism, but which also could be termed "contemplative science." In particular, the Platonic tradition is entirely ignored by Katz and barely touched on by Forman, yet it is in fact the center of this contemplative tradition. What characterizes this tradition, broadly speaking, is movement from dualistic to nondualistic consciousness as exemplified in the paradigmatic description of transcendence in Dionysius the Areopagite, in many respects akin to the Buddhist tradition of *prajnaparamita* or transcendent wisdom consciousness/recognition of emptiness.

It is important to note that Katz's constructivism is part and parcel of the much larger anti-Platonic movement that took place over the last quarter of the twentieth century into the early twenty-first. The broad if largely unexamined consensus derives from basic misunderstandings or misinterpretations of what Platonism actually is, as well as from the ascendency and ultimately the hegemony of leftism and materialism in the modern academy. By "leftism," I mean variants of Marxist or Marxian thought, characterized by materialism; economic or economic-political determinism; quasireligious belief in progress, even a near millennialism; animosity toward religion in general; a rejection of social hierarchy and tradition; and an animosity toward Platonism.

Such a general consensus is visible in the vast majority of critical theorists, but here I would like to focus on one figure in academic philosophy in order to illustrate in a little more detail what I mean. That figure is Richard Rorty (1931–2007), well known for his antifoundationalist or antiessentialist perspective as a "pragmatist" in the tradition of John Dewey. Antifoundationalism or antiessentialism predominated in the academic world of critical theory, which cut across many fields or disciplines, and the basic notion is that truth, or "truth" or any universal either is not worth searching for or does not exist at all. What does exist, in this perspective, is what is humanly created through language or cultural construct; in other words, truth is, in the words of Rorty, "not a goal of inquiry." Hence "*No theory of the nature of truth is possible*. It is only the relative about which there is anything to say [italics in original]."[31]

Now the first thing to observe about the pronouncement of Rorty, "no theory of the nature of truth is possible," concerns its *ex cathedra* nature. This dogmatism is not limited to Rorty alone; it is characteristic of antifoundationalism or antiessentialism as well as anti-Platonism more generally. That is, when one begins to search for the logical bases, the refutations of Platonism in the works that produce such pronouncements, one is surprised to find that they are not there. Rather, Rorty *begins* with instinctively antifoundational and anti-Platonic views, which he then explicates.

In a late work, Rorty, who was primarily in academic philosophy, delves into the area of religion, and here we see an example of what I am describing at work. In "Anticlericalism and Atheism" Rorty asserts that "the most important movements in twentieth-century philosophy have been anti-essentialist. These movements have mocked the ambitions of their predecessors . . . [to seek to] sift out the changing appearances from the enduringly real." He lists among the "mockers" Jacques Derrida, Bas van Fraassen, John Dewey, and Ludwig Wittgenstein, and after a number of digressions, he observes that one should "give up the idea that either the quest for truth or the quest for God is hard-wired into all human organisms"[32] and allow that "both are matters of cultural formation," after which the privatization of religion in the modern era seems to him quite natural.[33]

And then Rorty outlines his agenda for religion in the future. Rorty tells us that "holiness" does not reside "in a past event" but rather "only in an ideal future." Rorty then tells us that "my sense of the holy, insofar as I have one, is bound up with the hope that someday, any millennium now, my remote descendants will live in a global civilization where love is the only law." In this future society, "communication would be domination-free, class and caste would be unknown, hierarchy would be a matter of temporary pragmatic convenience, and power would be entirely at the disposal of the free agreement of a literate and well-educated electorate."[34] In a subsequent conversation with Gianni Vattimo, Rorty and Santiago Zabala seek to assert instead of "metaphysics" what they call "weak thought" and "conversation," and Rorty claims that "cutting oneself off from the metaphysical Logos is pretty much the same thing as ceasing to look for power and instead being content with charity."[35]

Allow me to unpack this just a bit. The first point is that for Rorty, "religion" and "holiness" are a progressive social project, a kind of sublimated millennialism along Marxian lines that aims toward an "ideal future." The second point is that this future is delineated in more or less strictly social terms; that is, he and his interlocutor seek to cut themselves off a "metaphysical Logos" (more a Christian than a Platonic term in this context) which they identify with "power" (meaning presumably political/institutional power) in favor of "communication," in a nonhierarchic, caste and class-free egalitarian system driven by "charity," presumably a pragmatic socialism or communism, though Rorty elsewhere says he's given up on both socialism and capitalism.[36] We could describe Rorty's thoughts here as reflecting a contemporary soft Marxism, that is, the political correctness of the time. And the same may be said of his book *Achieving Our Country: Leftist Thought in Twentieth-Century America* (1998).[37]

The reason I have spent a little time here on Rorty is that he exemplifies a broad intellectual tendency of the period, by no means yet gone, that seeks to wave away Platonism and the entire tradition of Platonic mysticism with a mere gesture. In this way of thinking, all one need do is be a "mocker," that is, to assert that "essentialism" is bad, that Platonism is what it is manifestly not, and to propose instead variant forms of social welfare and vaguely egalitarian political reforms tied to a loosely millenarian progressivism. And that is what I find so surprising. There is no ground, no basis, other than bald assertion, for the broader intellectual context that produced a "constructivist" interpretation of mysticism and that seeks to reject Platonism and the entire tradition of Western mysticism without even making the slightest effort to actually understand it on its own terms.

What happened, during the middle half of the twentieth century, is that the study of mysticism separated from the study specifically of Christian mysticism and became comparativist. Comparativism means that one seeks, as we saw in a transitional stage in the works of William James and Richard Bucke, to define mysticism in general terms as a human phenomenon characterized by x, y, and z and thus to be able to largely ignore the tradition I am terming Platonic mysticism. Cross-cultural comparison, particularly of very disparate religious traditions, makes it much easier to make claims of very different types concerning the category "mysticism," but it also disconnects those claims from the specifics of particular traditions, and in particular, of the tradition of Platonic mysticism.

Likewise, in *The Serpent's Gift*, Jeffrey Kripal refers to mysticism as represented by a doubled mode of consciousness.[38] But what is the nature of the mysticism about which he is writing? In *Roads of Excess, Palaces of Wisdom*, he does present a shorthand version of the history of Platonic mysticism in a chapter on Evelyn Underhill, referring to the Greek mystery religions, offers a wonderful quotation from Plotinus ("Shut your eyes and . . . evoke another way of seeing which everyone has but few use"), and observes that this Platonic mysticism "entered Christian intellectual history, winding its way through the centuries."[39] But that's about it for Platonic mysticism; here, as in the work of Forman, Hinduism is the main reference point. In

Forman's case, it was TM; in Kripal's, it is Tantra. And in the works of various figures on which each chapter focuses—Evelyn Underhill (Christianity), Louis Massignon (Sufism), R. C. Zaehner (Zoroastri-anism/Roman Catholicism), Agehananda Bharati (Hinduism), and Elliot Wolfson (Judaism)—all writers on various kinds of comparative mysticism, we find Platonic mysticism hardly mentioned at all.

Another example of scholarly disconnection from the specific history of Platonic mysticism is Randall Studstill's *The Unity of Mystical Traditions: The Transformation of Consciousness in Tibetan and German Mysticism* (2005). Studstill's book reveals exceptional erudition: he has read very widely in the study of mysticism, and having assimilated the full range of arguments in the field, he went so far as to create his own theoretical model of "mystical pluralism" based in "systems analysis" that seeks to analyze the cognitive aspects of mystical experience, thereby seeking also to reconcile the heterogeneity of mystical traditions with what he argues is their fundamental unity. It is quite interesting, then, with such a provocative and in some respects sympathetic thesis, he spends less than one page referring to the tradition of Platonic mysticism—in a book centered at least half on Meister Eckhart. Studstill does mention the vital importance of Platonism as mediated through Dionysius the Areopagite for Meister Eckhart.[40] But he is far more concerned with situating his book in relation to other contemporary scholarly models than in relation to the tradition that produced Meister Eckhart.

We can readily understand why this is so—the same is true of nearly all the mainstream academic discourse on mysticism by the early twenty-first century. As authors like Stace and before him, Jones, receded into the historical distance, so too did the tradition of Platonic mysticism, in its place the new comparativism based, for the most part, on models that seek to incorporate into the category "mysticism" all the world's religious traditions: Buddhism, Taoism, Hinduism, Christianity, Judaism, Islam, Native American. This is as true of Katz and those who accede to his constructivist agenda as it is of Forman; it is even true of Kripal, though his work is distinguished by his expression of doubts about antiessentialism and by his sympathy for the work of Mircea Eliade. On the whole, by the early twenty-first century, with a few exceptions of specialists in authors like Dionysius the Areopagite, "mysticism" seemed to be everything *but* Platonic mysticism.

It isn't that Platonic mysticism completely vanished; rather, it's that with comparativism, it so receded into the distance as to become just another allusion, often an inaccurate one. Thus, in *Mysticism* (1981), William Wainwright refers to Dionysius the Areopagite only as one among lists of mystics from different religions, and he paren- thetically misinterprets Dionysian metaphysics as dualistic.[41] That can happen because Platonic mysticism is, in this new world of compara- tivism, reduced to a series of minor individual examples disconnected from one another, Shankaracarya next to Ibn Arabi, Meister Eckhart next to mescaline. And this is true even of a book as sophisticated as *The Participatory Turn* (2008), whose authors develop a new com- parativist participatory model for understanding mysticism. For them, too, Platonic mysticism is only one among many reference points.[42]

Likewise, Anthony Steinbock, in *Phenomenology and Mysticism: The Verticality of Religious Experience* (2015), discusses mysticism in the "Abrahamic" traditions of Judaism, Christianity, and Islam, with a single exemplar for each—Theresa of Avila, Dov Baer, and Ruzbi- han Baqli.[43] Steinbock provides a rudimentary directional framework, emphasizing "verticality" over horizontal time and arguing that mysti- cism is best understood in terms of "experience." "Experience," of course, means a subject's mystical experience of the "givenness" of a divine object: in other words, the language and analysis is dualistic, so it is perhaps not surprising that the book does not mention or take into account Plato, Platonism, Neoplatonism, or the great exemplars of apophatic mysticism from Dionysius the Areopagite to Eckhart to *The Cloud of Unknowing*. None of these appear in the index or text. Here again, Platonic mysticism is completely eclipsed.

There have been a few authors who sought to understand Pla- tonic mysticism in several different contexts, often that of perennial philosophy. One of the better works written on perennial philosophy is Jonathan Shear's article "On Mystical Experiences as Support for Perennial Philosophy."[44] Shear surveys some of the authors we've already alluded to, including Katz and Forman, as well as Stace and some others, in order to develop the thesis that mystical experience is central to understanding perennial philosophy as well as the chal- lenges it poses. In particular, Shear calls into question Huston Smith's assertion that perennial philosophy rests more on "deduction," "pure intellection," and "metaphysical intuition" than on mystical experi- ence.[45] Shear points out, citing the author of *The Cloud of Unknowing* as well as Dionysius the Areopagite, that there is a tradition of an "empirically qualityless" experience that "transcends" thoughts and perceptions and that gave "rise to perennial philosophy in the first place."[46] Shear is correct to say that the concept "self" can open up into what is indescribable, and that indescribable transcendence is at the center of perennial philosophy, as it is to "philosophy as a rite of rebirth."[47] Shear clearly grasps an important aspect of this book's argument.

And in fact recent books give rise to much hope concerning the future study of consciousness, especially the books of B. Alan Wallace. The most important book on consciousness, close in many respects to Shear's article, is B. Alan Wallace, *Contemplative Science: Where Buddhism and Neuroscience Converge*. In it, Wallace (a long-time practitioner of Vajrayana Buddhism) describes how Buddhism (with a particular eye to Dzogchen) provides a much more developed and profound approach to consciousness than recent neuroscientific approaches. Wallace does not seem to have overmuch familiarity with the Western contemplative tradition on which we've relied in this book and shies away from terms like "perennial philosophy" because he is coming from a specifically Buddhist perspective.

Wallace establishes the terrain better than anyone else. For instance, he corrects the assertions of modern academic philosophers like John Searle, who offer pronouncements like this: "The idea that there might be a special method of investigating consciousness, namely 'introspection,' which is supposed to be a kind of inner observation, was domed to failure from the start, and it is not surprising that intro-spective psychology proved bankrupt."[48] Searle goes on to remark that the study of mind (by means of discursive reason alone) leaves those in academic philosophy "confused" and "in disagreement."[49] And no doubt it does. Wallace conclusively shows that such pronouncements can only take place in the absence of any familiarity with the long and rich history of Buddhist analysis of consciousness, in particular of its development of attentional practices, but also of teachings concerning primordial consciousness in Vajrayana Buddhism.

Wallace offers an excellent overview of the intersection of Buddhist meditation practice and neuroscience, but he also touches on Western European religion, and in particular the history of Platonism. He approvingly cites John Scotus Eriugena's writings on mystical experience, with good reason, and he mentions in passing Pythago-reanism and the ancient Mysteries, as well as Meister Eckhart, but these are figures and areas that call out for deeper and wider analysis.[50] Authors such as Meister Eckhart, the author of *The Cloud of Unknow-ing*, Jacob Böhme, and Emerson, to name a few, offer far more than passing remarks suggest. Even Plotinus merits only a passing allusion. At the same time, while Platonic mysticism was not the point of Wallace's book, he virtually alone among contemporary scholars has recognized the vital importance of these authors.

Wallace raises some striking points. In remarking on similarities between Buddhism, Neoplatonism, Vedanta, and Christian, Islamic, and Jewish mysticisms, he wonders aloud whether "this apparent commonality can be attributed to mere coincidence or to the historical propagation of a single, speculative metaphysical theory through South Asia and the Near East."[51] That would be the concept of perennial philosophy as it is often understood. But then he wryly remarks on the thesis that underlies this book: "Plotinus declared that his theories were based on his own experiential insights, and similar claims have been made by many Buddhist, Christian, and Vedantin contemplatives. If these cosmogonies are indeed based upon valid introspective knowledge, then there may be some plausibility to their assertions that introspective inquiry can lead to knowledge of the ultimate ground of being."[52] The word "cosmogonies" is a bit misleading here, because these figures are concerned not with cosmology so much as metaphysics, but the central point leads inexorably, as he himself notes, to perennial philosophy. And as he notes, it is not in vogue, so he too is careful to only slyly allude to it and its implications.[53]

Wallace argues against various kinds of pernicious ideologies that he terms "idolatries." He critiques theological idolatries of God in theism or monotheism; he critiques the idolatry of the brain in neuroscience; he critiques the idolatry of theories based in discursive reason; and he concludes by critiquing even a possible grand convergence of Buddhism, Christian mysticism, and contemplative practices with neuroscience, because that too could become an idolatry. What he encourages instead is an "empirical approach."[54]

It is at least possible to envision a convergence with neuroscience of Buddhism, Christian mysticism, and other contemplative practices and experiential maps. One could imagine a larger synthesis, suggested for instance by Andrew Newberg in his coauthored book *The Mystical Mind*.[55] There, he proposes a theory that informs his later books, and that is a variant of perennial philosophy—essentially a Platonic hierarchy of consciousness culminating in the experience of subject-object transcendence. This culmination he refers to as "Absolute Unitary Being [AUB]." Of course, from the perspective of Platonic mysticism, the One is beyond being and cannot be expressed in conceptual terms except through negation, so from this perspective, the notion of Absolute Unitary Being is a lower or prior state to transcendence.

It is true, of course, that some scholars of mysticism continued to acknowledge and even focus on what we are here terming Platonic mysticism. Some exceptionally illuminating books include Andrew Louth, *The Origins of the Christian Mystical Tradition: From Plato to Denys* (1981), and Eric Perl, *Theophany: The Neoplatonic Philosophy of Dionysius the Areopagite*, (2007), to give two stellar examples.[56] Another is the monumental work of Bernard McGinn, whose *The Presence of God: A History of Christian Mysticism*, and in particular the first volume, *The Foundations of Christian Mysticism* (1991), offers many corrections to modern scholarship that emphasizes mystical experience as a category separate from its religious, philosophical, and theological context and seeks to recognize the Platonic dimensions of Christian mysticism.[57] Platonism is crucial for understanding the historical development of Christian mysticism, and scholarship on this subject undoubtedly will continue. If Platonic mysticism went into eclipse for a short period of a few decades, there is reason to believe that the eclipse is now passing.

CHAPTER FOUR

The Externalist Fallacy

As we have seen, the study of mysticism is largely out of academic favor today, and Platonic mysticism has been in almost total eclipse. So when, in the late twentieth century, an entire new academic field was born, which came to call itself "Western esotericism," one would think that it would certainly feature or at least include mysticism, since on the face of it, one can hardly see what could better qualify as esoteric religion than mysticism. But this was not to be. In fact, mysticism was often excluded from the gerrymandered, for the most part ill-defined area of "Western esotericism," and more broadly remains out of favor in much of the academic study of religion even today. In what follows, we are going to explore in detail some examples of how mysticism is frequently shunned or ignored, even in the putative field of "esotericism," with particular attention to what I term "the externalist fallacy."

To begin, we might remark that it is not only mysticism that is out of contemporary academic favor, but also Platonism and especially Neoplatonism. Given my argument that mysticism cannot be clearly understood without reference to Platonism, it only makes sense that these two areas, which overlap, should have both been relegated to a back closet. Plotinus in particular embodies the intersection of Platonism and mysticism, and for the most part Plotinus is not studied or taught. Among my own students over the past several decades, even philosophy majors, I have yet to encounter a single one who had even heard Plotinus's name, let alone read his works. Only rarely does one encounter a faculty member whose work even tangentially refers to Plotinus. Nationally and even internationally, there are only a small number of scholars that specialize in mysticism or, for that matter, Platonism.

But what I want to look at here are the claims or arguments that some scholars have used in order to explicitly seek to dismiss or exclude these subjects from the academic world. This is a categorically stronger exclusion than simply omission. Omission is comparatively benign, but what we need to look closely at is actually closer to malign: it is the attempted exclusion of whole areas of religious study, as well as of particular approaches to the study of religion. In particular, we will look at the language and rationale for such exclusions, which, as one might expect, share some features. What we are considering here is much stronger than simply ignoring mysticism: it is academics seeking to excommunicate those who study and take seriously the category "mysticism." This is a relatively new phenomenon, and one that bears some scrutiny.

I do not wish to survey the whole of antimystical scholarship here. But I do want to consider some of the main arguments presented against mysticism and Platonism and excavate some of their infrastructure. For as we shall see, the invectives that we find against the academic study of mysticism reveal some contemporary biases that are important to recognize. It has become commonplace for many in the field of religious studies to reject or even denounce the work of Mircea Eliade, and the reason for this is, as Daniel Dubuisson puts it in his bitter invective against Eliade, that Eliade relied upon three unacceptable sources, all mingled together: "a Platonic one, understood in its widest sense" as including such figures as "Plotinus, Proclus, Meister Eckhart, Nicholas of Cusa, [and] Marsilio Ficino," as well as "Hermeticism," and "all the mystic gnoseologies and all the forms of esotericism that so fascinated Eliade."[1] All of this is, for Dubuisson, so unacceptable as to produce a sustained fury directed at Eliade through many pages of denunciation.[2]

What is it that so incenses Dubuisson about Eliade? It is that Eliade's thought is informed by Platonism and, from a Christian perspective, is "pagan and heretical,"[3] which is also to say "irrational," because like phenomenology in general, it is "more mystical than philosophical" and accepts the notion of "pure intuitive knowledge that only deals with what transcends particular historical conditions."[4] All of these ideas or perspectives are subjected to withering scorn.

Dubuisson is highly critical of the great scholar of religion Mircea Eliade, as has become customary, but Eliade is only symptomatic for Dubuisson of the greater problem. That greater problem, as Dubuisson makes clear in *The Western Construction of Religion: Myths, Knowledge, and Ideology* (*L'Occident et la religion: Mythes, science et idéologie* [1998]) is Platonism, mysticism, or esoteric religion; because "admitting a priori that the intelligible transcends the sensible" "is an attitude incompatible with the aims of an authentic, well-founded scientific undertaking." Furthermore, Dubuisson proclaims, "the intelligible no less than the perceptible belongs to this world, and both are the issue of comparable historical processes." "Both are exactly situated on the same level, the human level."[5] These are, needless to say, *ex cathedra* proclamations by Dubuisson that do not require logical explication or evidence.

Dubuisson rejects "mystic experience," "the direct, lived experience of the individual confronted with the dazzling revelation of a superior reality" because any assertion of a "transcendent level" of "lived, religious experience" "brings in its wake the indispensable but inadmissible epistemological corollary that the substratum of this experience escapes history, that it cannot be assigned to any of the domains (sociological, psychological, etc.) among which are distributed our knowledge and our explanations of human facts."[6] On the one hand are "materialist thinkers" (among whom scholars of religion must be numbered, according to Dubuisson), and on the other are "all those (Platonists, Christians, esoterics, mystics) who subordinate the existence of this human world to principles that transcend it and to which 'religious facts' testify."[7] Because when one insists dogmatically that all religion must be understood as a "human construct," one is in fact not only including what is permissible to study (discourse communities, objects, and so forth) but also excluding what is impermissible (which Dubuisson helpfully names for us as Platonism, esoteric religion, and mysticism).

Now one might think that this kind of invective is a bit eccentric, that is, outside the mainstream of the academic study of religion, because it is rhetorically extreme. But it does reflect a widespread dismissal of Eliade's work and premises, as well as of what is often glibly termed "the essentialist fallacy." Of course, as I have pointed out elsewhere, even though it has become *de rigueur* to issue a disclaimer that one is by no means "essentialist," actually when one traces the concept back, there is nowhere any convincing argument that "essentialism" actually describes Platonism or mysticism, or even if it did, that its presence is a fallacy. It is not enough to simply assert *ex cathe-*

dra that "essentialism" is a "fallacy," because pronouncing something to be false is not the same as actually proving that it is so. In fact, "essentialism" is just a word that might be held to refer to an aspect of Platonism; it refers not to a fallacy but to a philosophical viewpoint that happened not to be in vogue in the early twenty-first century. It is also interesting how, in *Twentieth Century Mythologies*, Dubuisson contrasts confessional Christianity with mysticism and Platonism, which in the manner of the most condemnatory of the anti-Nicene Fathers like Tertullian, he regards as "heretical." In other words, and this is quite interesting, the materialistic, this-worldly arch-hater of all things Platonic, Hermetic, and mystical is in fact reflecting and transmitting a Christian heresy-hunting agenda that long predates him.

Now it is one thing if someone from a dogmatically religious perspective—and probably some ignorance of the actual subjects themselves—condemns Platonism, mysticism, or esoteric religion as heretical, but it is something entirely different when the one doing the condemning seems to be a modern, secular academic. When one sees a modern secular academic replicating the heresiophobia of confessional Christianity in late antiquity, one has to wonder what, exactly, is going on. And in fact there is an interesting dimension to such a case, but to see it, we need to turn to another academic author on these subjects, in this instance, one whose work centers on the newly developed category of "Western esotericism."

The term "Western esotericism" has been used to demarcate various, somewhat different areas of inquiry, sometimes harking back to late antiquity, but in other definitions often centering on the early modern period and such movements or currents of thought and practice as Hermeticism, Rosicrucianism, alchemy, magic, and Christian theosophy in the tradition of Jacob Böhme. These in particular were marked as "Western esotericism" by Antoine Faivre, holder of a chair in the field at the Sorbonne for many years, and in many respects the founding figure for inquiry into this new academic field.[8] Over several decades, the field developed considerably, with an endowed chair in Hermetic philosophy and related currents at the University of Amsterdam, and a second endowed chair in Western esotericism held by Nicholas Goodrick-Clarke at the University of Exeter, followed by the development of academic organizations, the Association for the Study of Esotericism, and then the European Society for the Study of Western Esotericism, which hold conferences in alternating years, as well as sections at the American Academy of Religion and the

International Association for the History of Religion. After a relatively short time, a couple of decades, it seemed "Western esotericism" had arrived in academia.

But what, exactly, had arrived? This is an interesting question, more interesting than one might at first realize. As I have detailed elsewhere, the field of "Western esotericism" from the beginning took on, particularly in Europe, a certain gerrymandered look. Some things were included as esoteric, while others were excluded, and the category "exoteric" (the antonym of "esoteric" and presumably crucial to understanding it) was rigorously ignored. Above all, the subjects of mysticism and Platonism were largely excluded (though not entirely from the American conferences of the Association for the Study of Esotericism). And one has to ask, why would mysticism be excluded from the domain of esoteric religion? Wouldn't mysticism be the exemplar par excellence? Certainly one would think so: after all, Jacob Böhme, typically classified as a mystic, is central to the Faivrean model of what constitutes Western esotericism, and virtually no one in the presumed field would deny that Böhme belongs there. Yet mysticism is almost completely excluded.

One of the more interesting and paradoxical cases of scholarship on esotericism is that of Wouter Hanegraaff, who as noted earlier, holds a chair in the field of Western esotericism at the University of Amsterdam. In a series of publications, Hanegraaff has developed an invective against what he terms "religionism," which he defines as "the project of exploring historical sources in search of what is eternal and universal."[9] Hanegraaff opposes to "religionism" (evidently his bête noir) a "*methodology* of historical criticism combined with a *theoretical focus* on the manifold effects of the encounter between Hellenistic paganism and biblical traditions [italics in original]."[10] And where is the paradigm for this "empirical" approach to be found? In the anti-esoteric polemics of Jacob Thomasius (1622–1684), Ehregott Daniel Colberg (1659–1698), and Johann Jacob Brucker (1696–1700), who represented "exactly the right combination" for the study of "Western esotericism."[11] Thomasius, Colberg, and Brucker emphasized how confessional Christianity (represented by biblical Protestantism) had been polluted periodically by the "falsehoods" and "superstition" of paganism. The job of the scholar, in their eyes, was to separate the wheat (rationalism and Protestantism allow us to see the wheat) from the chaff (paganism, Platonism, Hermetism, and the like). Hence Brucker wrote that the Neoplatonists "hatched all kinds of books, as scandalous and harmful miscarriages of their weird brains, and put them as strange eggs into the nest of the ancient philosophers."[12] The heart of the problem is that such groups' views, including the Christian theosophers in the tradition of Böhme, "are based not on the light of reason but on claims of internal, divine illumination."[13]

Now it might seem strange that a modern scholar of religion would find an ideal precedent in polemical, heresiophobic authors like these, whose works are actually more or less diatribes against their subjects. But Hanegraaff says that what matters is that they represent the ancestors of modern historical criticism and rationalism. It is perhaps worth noting here that Wouter Hanegraaff's father was a Protestant minister and theologian and that one of the most prominent American evangelical authors is in fact Hanegraaff's relative, Hank Hanegraaff, who has produced antiesoteric, antioccult resources online, derived from a combination of, yes, biblical Protestantism (he is known as the "Bible Answer Man") and opposition to what he perceives as irrational or demonically inspired superstition.

In a subsequent work, *Western Esotericism: A Guide for the Perplexed*, we find the application of what Hanegraaff began to develop in the earlier book. As an introduction to Western esotericism and a "guide for the perplexed," this book is quite strange, because at its center is not a presence but an absence. "Western esotericism" is not clearly demarcated at all, and the neophyte would have little idea what to make of an area of study defined primarily as "the academy's dustbin of rejected knowledge" that, although it is not "just a random collection of discarded materials without any further connection," presents "no such thing as a 'best example' of esotericism." Indeed, "there are no prototypical 'esotericists.' "[14] Hanegraaff's approach "begs the question of definition and demarcation," yet it "assumes that the field *as a whole* [italics in original] can be set apart as somehow different from other fields of inquiry."[15] His best definition is that Western esotericism is "characterized by a strong emphasis on specific worldviews and epistemologies that are at odds with normative post-Enlightenment intellectual culture."[16] But that, of course, could be just about anything.

Early in this book, Hanegraaff rejects what he terms "religionism" as an approach to Western esotericism and claims that such a model "rests upon the conviction [of the scholar] that a universal, hidden, esoteric dimension of reality really does exist."[17] He goes on to assert that "scholarly methods . . . are 'exoteric' by definition and can only study what is empirically available to observers." What is more, "all that scholars can do is study the beliefs, convictions, or theories that have been formulated *about* [the Absolute], but as scholars they are not qualified to assess their truth or falsity." In fact, with regard to transcendent aspects of consciousness, "we simply do not know—and cannot know."[18] Later, he asserts "from a historical perspective, religionism makes the mistake of ignoring religious diversity, historical change, and any question of 'external' influences because all it cares about is an experiential dimension that transcends history and will always remain inaccessible to scholarly research by definition."[19]

Now there are several problems with these sweeping generalizations about so-called "religionists." We begin with the bizarre nature of the term itself. Only in the study of religion is such a term possible as a pejorative. By contrast, in physics for instance, is the term "physicist" a pejorative? The idea would be ridiculous on its face. How then can "religionist" be constructed as pejorative for someone who studies religion? The mere existence of the term used in this way reveals that there must be a peculiar underlying problem it conceals. And there is. But the problem is on the part of the label-giver. Effectively, the coining of the term is itself a religious statement—its user seeks to emphatically exclude from the study of esoteric religion any perspective that is "tainted" by—esoteric religion itself. Paradoxically, however, this would mean that the scholar must "always" remain outside esoteric religion (that is, always be an externalist). And even beyond such a claim is Hanegraaff's theological assertion that scholars are by definition limited or truncated human beings who "cannot know" because participatory experience is "inaccessible to scholarly research." Such a claim is belied by the history of anthropological research, for instance, which has a much more sophisticated set of approaches to insider/outsider issues.

It is worth remarking on that Hanegraaff, in his sweeping generalizations about "religionist" scholars, engages in rather extreme reductionism and falsification. For example, he claims that my book *Wisdom's Children: A Christian Esoteric Tradition* is an example of suspect "religionism."[20] Hence, he claims, I am "ignoring religious diversity, historical change, and any question of 'external' influences because all [my work] cares about is an experiential dimension that transcends history."[21] But this is manifestly untrue. In reality, *Wisdom's Children* is a book about the history of the Christian theosophical tradition in the school of Jacob Böhme. It is about the major figures and texts in the tradition that includes Jacob Böhme, John Pordage, and a number of other historical figures. It is about Christian theosophy, pure and simple. Furthermore, it concentrates on the unique nature of the Christian theosophical tradition, which (as I point out in the conclusion) bears some similarity to some aspects of Gnosticism in late antiquity and which inherits many prior esoteric currents, including alchemy and astrology, as well as Platonic mysticism. It is very clearly a distinct school on which the book focuses.

But in *Wisdom's Children*, I do describe in detail the accounts by early modern authors Böhme, Pordage, Leade, and others of their mystical experiences. In other words, the book does describe, without casting aspersions on the authors discussed, their experiential accounts. Were I to remove this aspect of the book, it would be as if the book were decapitated; it would no longer give the reader a sense of the theosophical tradition from the perspective of theosophers, but rather would only give names, dates, and data. It would become an *externalist* work, of limited value at best for understanding theosophy itself. From this example, we can begin to see what I have come to term the "externalist fallacy."

What authors like Dubuisson and Hanegraaff assert is a radical externalism. Hanegraaff claims that the "experiential dimension that transcends history. . . . will always remain inaccessible to scholarly research by definition."[22] The scholar, he alleges, must always remain outside, removed from the subject. But this is a modern version of the Protestant antiesoteric rhetoric of the early modern era, in which a desiccated rationalism rejects whatever has the "taint" of the mystical or transcendent, exactly what his models Thomasius, Colberg, and Brucker did, but in a new context, that of contemporary academia. To make the subject matter, "esotericism," palatable in a modern academic context, in other words, exactly that which makes it esoteric, its assertion of an inner esoteric dimension of reality accessed through particular esoteric practices, ironically has to be rejected or left out of one's scholarly narrative.

This is a naïve view, of course. Contemporary anthropology, for example, has long since accepted that an "insider" account complements that of an "outsider" academic perspective, that the two can go together, and that in fact only an insider/outsider account that includes both perspectives can do justice to a particular religious tradition. To give an example, scholarship on Tantric Buddhism that does not include an insider's perspective, at least to some extent, is highly unlikely to provide an accurate view of the tradition. What appears from the outside to be one way may very well look quite different from the perspective of an initiate; what looks alarming, like mention of "killing an enemy," might actually refer to overcoming aspects of one's own emotional reactions.

Hanegraaff also refers not to the Platonic tradition, but rather to "Platonic Orientalism," a term that he draws from John Walbridge, much of whose work is dedicated to critique of the French scholar of esoteric Islam, Henry Corbin.[23] The term "orientalism" of course invokes the anticolonialist rhetoric of the late twentieth century as represented by Edward Said—and in this context it is, of course, a pejorative. An "orientalist" in this recent context is not so much a specialist in Asian religions as a European colonialist who projects views on the "other," typically referring to the "others" of the Middle East. Using the misleading term "Platonic Orientalism" to refer to Platonism and Hermetism in late antiquity and to Renaissance Platonism means that one does not have to engage the implications of a Platonic perspective, but rather can dismiss it as "orientalizing." Hanegraaff is aware that this is in fact misleading but claims that "for the present discussion it is not necessary to explore the nature of the relation between these two theoretical frameworks."[24] Aware of the problematic nature of the terminology, he employs it nonetheless not despite but *because* of the pejorative implications of "orientalism." By using it, Platonism and Platonic mysticism are not recognized and understood on their own terms, but externalized and thereby subtly dismissed as a form of "orientalism."

In fact, it is more than ironic for scholars on a subject such as esoteric religion to seek to exclude what is most esoteric about it, what we might describe as its upper register. What, after all, is esoteric about esoteric religion, if not that it includes dimensions that transcend conventional subject-object divisions? An externalist approach that relies only on historical reading and discursive analysis but that does not acknowledge initiatory aspects of the tradition is almost certainly not going to have access to the upper register of possibilities in it, nor is it likely to present it accurately or completely.

Other approaches are possible and, I would have to say, warranted. Jeffrey Kripal writes that he is "committed both to the most robust rational-critical methods *and* to the metaphysical reality that is the object (really, I suspect, the subject) of religious experience and expression."[25] Kripal goes on to remark that "the new questions I am led to ask after this empirical-historical scholarship are precisely the questions that Hanegraaff won't let me ask as a scholar." He continues: "Must we *all* restrict ourselves to historical issues? Must we *never* venture beyond historical-criticism and ask the philosophical questions that every sophomore in our classrooms is already asking?" It is possible to "define the intellectual life along strict historical and materialistic lines," he concludes, but "I am no longer willing to do this."[26] And he quotes approvingly Victoria Nelson, who writes that "the greatest taboo among serious intellectuals. . . . is the heresy of challenging a materialist worldview."[27]

It is entirely possible and indeed quite common and accepted not only in anthropology but also in the study of political groups to engage as an insider, thereby actually understanding one's subject, while at the same time maintaining a critical analytical perspective that strives for objectivity. To give an example, Dimitris Kitis, in a study of contemporary Greek radicalism, observes early on in a major article that one of his commitments "is to provide a participant perspective while maintaining an objective scholarly stance."[28] Kitis goes on to remark that he draws on personal anarchist accounts and interviews as well as personal observations, all of which provide "insider insight into the phenomenon" of contemporary anarchism. But were the equivalent of Hanegraaff's anti-insider caricature of "religionism" applied to this political scientist, what would the comparable term of attempted dismissal be: politicist, because he at once is both participant insider and critical outsider? It is clear Kitis is in fact seeking to maintain at once both an insider and an outsider perspective. His work is not polemical. So why should the study of religion along the same lines, an account that seeks to include the actual perspective of the subject, be condemned?

We ought to keep in mind the larger academic context in the humanities and social sciences. It is common in both areas that scholars express their own political sentiments through their scholarship. Thus, feminists are free to write engaged feminist scholarship; environmentalists typically write deeply engaged scholarship; Marxists or post-Marxists produce Marxist or Marxian scholarship; area studies, for instance, African or African American, Latino or Hispanic, and American Indian or Native American scholarship, often expresses clear commitments by a scholar. Likewise, scholarship on political radicalism, however much one might encourage an aspiration for objectivity, very frequently wears its commitments on its sleeve. A scholar writing on the French New Right can be so critical of his subject that the founder of the French New Right feels compelled to denounce the scholar's work.[29] Yet far less committed scholarship in the area of religion, scholarship that seeks to explore empathetically the nature of esoteric religion, is out of bounds? That seems more than strange.

The larger category here is "esoteric religion," to which mysticism belongs. Mysticism, especially apophatic mysticism, but kataphatic as well, focuses on subject-object transcendence either in vision (kataphatic) or in pure transcendence (apophatic). "Esoteric religion" includes mysticism, but it also includes alchemy, astrology, and magical traditions that may focus more on what I term "cosmological gnosis," which often entails an emphasis on effects in the cosmos, for instance, the transmutation of plant tinctures, minerals, or other substances. The broader category here is often termed "Western esotericism," but because this term is itself problematic for various reasons that I discuss in detail elsewhere, I am here simply using the term "esoteric religion."

There are a number of possible reasons why someone might attempt to advance such an exclusion of those approaches to esoteric religion that take it seriously on its own terms. One is the Christian inheritance of the heresy/orthodoxy divide from late antiquity through the medieval and early modern periods. Heresiophobia, as I detailed in *The New Inquisitions*, has a long history in the West and did not disappear with the emergence of modern secularity; rather, it manifested in new, more secularized forms.[30] As Kripal indicated, one of those forms is an enduring strain of scientific materialism that privileges only discursive rationalism, and for which all the various aspects of esoteric religion—mysticism, cosmological traditions, the paranormal—are anathema and relegated to the large trash can typically marked as "the irrational." This is still true despite those theories and findings of contemporary physics that seem to brush up against and even overlap what we would term esoteric religion.

Another motivation for attempting to exclude esoteric religion as discussed in this book from the study of "esotericism" has to do with academic "respectability." Esoteric religion historically has been ignored, or marginalized, and the expressed goal of some scholars has been to get "esotericism" established as a field in the academy. To make the study of esoteric religion fit into the contemporary academy and its predilections, it is the easiest course to seek to excise those aspects, like Platonic mysticism, that challenge prevailing worldviews. Thus, even though esoteric religion can be itself vaguely defined as "characterized by a strong emphasis on specific worldviews and epistemologies that are at odds with normative post-Enlightenment intellectual culture," scholarship that takes seriously the implications of such a challenge is to be excluded.[31] If so, then in the name of "academic respectability," exactly what is esoteric about esoteric religion is excluded, making the field into a kind of ironically empty exercise.

But whatever the motivations of externalist scholars—who sometimes seem as vitriolic as reductionist militant atheists—the fact remains that their work rests on a fallacy. This fallacy is that one can do justice to esoteric religion from an exoteric perspective. As Peter Kingsley put it, "there is no entrance to the esoteric from the outside."[32] What makes esoteric religion esoteric is that it is based in cosmological or metaphysical gnosis.[33] Cosmological gnosis refers to those esoteric traditions, like alchemy or magic, that center on this-worldly aims through a partial transcendence of subject-object division. Thus, for instance, in an alchemical operation, the operator seeks to effect a transmutation of a substance, but there is also an inner symbolic and conscious dimension to the work. Likewise, magic and astrology are cosmological and based in hidden correspondences between us and the cosmos beyond us. Metaphysical gnosis centers on pure transcendence of subject-object divisions, such as that found exemplified in the apophatic mysticism of Plotinus, Dionysius the Areopagite, or Meister Eckhart. These exist on a spectrum, from exoteric subject-object dualism, as in modern materialistic rationalism, through partial transcendence of subject-object dualism (cosmological gnosis, sometimes termed magic) to complete transcendence of subject-object dualism (metaphysical gnosis, sometimes termed mysticism).

Now if one insists on excluding anything other than historical data and rejects out of hand Platonic, Hermetic, mystical, or esoteric perspectives themselves, as well as any possibility of comprehending timelessness or transcendence, then esoteric religion on this spectrum will remain inaccessible. And as a result, one will not be able to say anything meaningful about esoteric religion itself. One could pedantically describe the outer lineaments of and historical data concerning esoteric religion, but if one has to stop short of entering into the perspective at hand, then one simply cannot understand it, precisely because it *is* esoteric. The externalist fallacy is to believe that what is most meaningful can be understood only through external discursive analysis, as if one sought to realize the beauty of a magnificent Hudson River School landscape painting through analysis of its chemical content. Historical or other kinds of data are of value, no doubt of that; my own scholarship is historically grounded, and indeed, I suppose somewhat ironically, in contrast to Hanegraaff's own introduction to the subject, my introduction to Western esoteric religion is primarily a historical survey. But to understand what is esoteric about esoteric religion, one also has to empathetically enter into one's subject. There is no way to properly grasp it from without, like some self-appointed inquisitor; data provides no means of deeper comprehension. The word "esoteric" has an antonym, after all: exoteric. Externalism means to attempt to dogmatically insist on exoteric means to describe what is esoteric, that is, fully understood only from the inside.

Ultimately, the study of esoteric religion is the study of different levels or kinds of consciousness and of its transcendence. The word "consciousness" refers to awareness both of what is perceived outside us and of our own mind and awareness itself. Thus the word "consciousness" implies a dualism between that which perceives and that which is perceived. Esoteric religion is esoteric precisely because it is about the ascent of consciousness from a crude subject-object dualism toward ever-subtler awareness of how, in higher levels of consciousness, the subject-object division does not hold; what is within mirrors what is without, and as the Emerald Tablet of Hermetic tradition has it, "as above, so below." Thus, alchemy is a tradition of working with laboratory substances—mineral, plant, or animal—but also of working with their inner aspects. Likewise, astrology engages in the analysis of planetary and constellations' meanings, which are simultaneously outer and inner principles. Mysticism can include kataphatic visionary phenomena (in which what is "external" is at the same time "internal"), but ultimately it goes beyond that into metaphysical gnosis, which is the apophatic transcendence of self-other divisions. The ascent of consciousness is what makes esoteric religion esoteric; if it is not present, then what you are looking at is not esoteric religion.

A militantly externalist approach to esoteric religion cannot shed light on its subject because it approaches it from the dualistic and limited perspective of a discursive rationality that confines itself only to historical and materialistic data and refuses to acknowledge the subtle nature of its subject. The externalist fallacy is to believe that one can accurately convey or depict esoteric religion from outside, without respecting the fact that esoteric religious traditions allude to changes in consciousness. It sheds no light on anything to attempt to toss Platonism, Hermetism, and mysticism into a trashcan labeled "irrationality," as those like Dubuisson seek to do, or by pretending that one can excommunicate from scholarship those whose approaches and perspectives differ from one's own limited or confused presuppositions. Externalism is a dead end. Its approaches leave us stranded on the outside.

Of course the changes in consciousness signaled by esoteric texts and images can be discussed by and are not incompatible with discursive reason and analysis. The great religious philosopher Plotinus devotes much of his *Enneads* to exactly such an endeavor, seeking to describe and analyze discursively the subtler aspects of his inner experiences and their implications. Engaging with the tradition we seek to understand, engaging with the texts and images and coming to understand them on their own terms, while maintaining our own analytical perspective—and only such engagement—enables us to more deeply and fully comprehend the nature of esoteric religion. The next chapter we will explore the nature of the model I am presenting, a theory that integrates our understanding of both literature and mystical literature.

CHAPTER FIVE

On Literature and Mysticism

In *Restoring Paradise: Western Esotericism, Literature, Art, and Consciousness*, I developed the broad outlines of a theory about how Western esoteric religion was chiefly transmitted by way of literature and art. There, I demonstrated through a series of examples that some literary works can be understood as having esoteric dimensions and as initiatory means. Not all literature or art, of course, but some can certainly be best understood as bearing initiatory significances. These esoteric works, I held, may be understood as having what I termed *hieroeidetic* meaning: that is, through particular forms of language and image, the reader encounters the hieratic or revenant figure or form through "the field of imagination midway between the mundane and the transcendent." "Hieroeidetic knowledge exists in the field of knower and known, where a [revelatory] encounter may take place."[1] Here, I am going to continue to develop this as part of a larger theoretical understanding of literature, in particular, mystical literature.

To begin, we must return to Platonism, which is the *fons et origo* of what we may call the West, meaning the extraordinary literary, artistic, and religious creativity of Western Europe, as well as of Western Europe in diaspora in the New World and in the Pacific East. Platonism, especially as manifested in the magnum opus of the tradition, Plotinus's *Enneads*, is at heart a contemplative tradition, and it is also experiential. It includes both aspects: direct contemplative experience and reflective analysis and explication. It is not "irrational," or "antirational," but eminently rational. However, it also includes an experiential contemplative dimension that recognizes what preoccupied the literary critic Northrop Frye at the end of his life: "the theme of the reality of the spiritual world."[2]

The sophisticated literary critic of today may be taken aback, perhaps even appalled by such a perspective as Frye's: how is it possible to write of "the reality of the spiritual world" with regard to literature? Aren't we entirely beyond that? After all, if the prevailing view in the academy can be described as a sardonic nihilism that privileges only a rarified discursive rationality and insists, as a whole array of perspectives do, on a kind of simplistic materialism as the foundation for whatever ideological superstructure is erected upon it, well then, "we" are not going to be investigating such subjects as "the reality of the spiritual world." Our assumptions preclude it.

The problem is that such assumptions as undergird poststructuralism, deconstruction, postmodernism, and "critical theory" concerning literature are fundamentally materialist and antimystical. Their genealogy is generally traceable back to Marx and various forms of Marxism. Almost across the board, the lineages run from Marx through the Frankfurt School to figures from Jacques Derrida and Julia Kristeva to Gilles Deleuze, Donna Harraway, Paul de Man, and many others. And there is another dimension to this genealogy, which is that from Marx and the Frankfurt School through to many prominent critical theorists' work, it tends to privilege the combative discursive rationalism that also governs philosophy and especially analytic philosophy. The implicit perspective is materialistic.

A similar perspective is implicit in what may be termed the "constructionist" interpretation of mystical literature in the late twentieth century. Championed by a number of modern scholars of mysticism, this perspective sought to erase mystical experience by claiming that mystical experience is "constructed" by the mystic as a result of cultural and social conditioning. This perspective is a little more sophisticated than the crude Marxist materialistic rejection of religion as a whole as the "opiate of the people" in that it recognizes the role that culture has in filtering or shaping what and how we understand and experience anything, including a mystical experience.

At the same time, by insisting on the "constructed" nature of all perspectives, constructionists paint themselves into a corner, because this view would logically mean that constructionism itself cannot provide a vantage point from which to objectively see and understand mystical experience—for a constructionist perspective itself is by definition also "constructed." Consequently, even though constructionists in general purport to make veridical claims about mystical experience, such claims cannot be any more objective than the mystical experiences that the constructionist claims to deconstruct.[3] And this is, of course, the dirty secret that is hidden in modern assertions of antimysticism and antiessentialism as well as anti-Platonism and anti-esoteric perspectives more broadly: that just because someone *claims* that a perspective is invalidated by their rhetoric does not make it so.

A more productive approach is "philosophical esotericism," which seeks to decode philosophical writing along the lines laid out by Leo Strauss. Those who pursue philosophical esotericism recognize that mysticism is a central part of what must be called esoteric philosophy, that Platonism and Hermeticism, and indeed the Western esoteric religiophilosophical inheritance as a whole often encodes what it means and requires deciphering.[4] But those who investigate philosophical esotericism in the manner of Strauss are not looking at mysticism. What they are looking at is what they interpret as rhetorical subterfuge behind which is "philosophical rationalism." In *Philosophy Between the Lines: The Lost Art of Esoteric Writing*, Arthur Melzer makes a good case for the existence of esoterically encoded rationalism in the works of such figures as Pierre Bayle, Denis Diderot, and René Descartes.[5] And one can readily believe that an encoded rationalism is to be found here and there among Western philosophical authors, as also among some religious authors. But that is certainly not the only kind of esoteric writing, if indeed it really qualifies as that at all, for as Melzer himself points out, mystical literature certainly qualifies; indeed, it is of mystical literature that one thinks first, when thinking of esoteric writing.

Of course, in order to begin to understand mystical literature, one has to at least provisionally inhabit or at least seek to inhabit the perspective it represents. Platonism, as I have outlined elsewhere, has an ontological hierarchy that, like Buddhism, is grounded in assertions about the true nature of reality. It is not enough to reject Platonism, mysticism, or Buddhism out of hand, as if by gesturing one can dispense with the claims concerning the true nature of reality at the center of the Platonic ontological hierarchy. One has to begin with the recognition that there may be in Platonic literature hints pointing toward an understanding that transcends but can be analyzed and to some extent described by discursive reason.

These hints in Platonic literature may be termed "esoteric writing" because they disclose, sometimes through allusion, sometimes metaphor, almost always through the indirection of dialogue, not only ontological but also meontic truths. The word "meontic" derives from the Greek ὄντος, or *ontos*, referring to being, but with the privative *me* added. The philosopher Nicholas Berdyaev used the word to refer, not to nonbeing in the sense of lack or absence in the way sometimes it is understood, but to the transcendence of being. Thus, in Berdyaev's usage, meontic refers to transcendent truths grounded in the source of freedom beyond being. This transcendent source, in Platonism, is called the One.

The One in the Platonic tradition is not suceptible to conceptual capture; language only points toward it, but it remains outside our subject-object discourse. Sara Rappe underscores this point in *Reading Neoplatonism*, when she remarks that "the identity theory of truth, the doctrine that intellect is identical with its objects," is the "foundation of the philosophical enterprise we know as Neoplatonism."[6] The Platonic tradition cannot be understood through the modern notion that truth is a product of discourse, because "this doctrine of intellectual, or unitive, knowing entails precisely that truth is not structured like language and is not a product of any discourse." Intellective truth is "not available for transmission in any discursive form."[7] The One is known directly by the intellect not as an object of knowledge, but rather, as Plotinus put it, "when the soul wishes to see the One by itself, it is just by being with it that it sees . . . because it is not other than that which is being known."[8]

Without this key, one cannot begin to understand the Platonic tradition either in Platonism proper (the tradition from Plato through Damascius) or in Christian mysticism in the tradition indebted to Dionysius the Areopagite. And the two traditions are in fact ultimately one, or at least, that was the conclusion of scholars of mysticism throughout the period from the nineteenth into the midtwentieth centuries. André-Jean Festugière puts it succinctly: "When the [Church] Fathers 'think' their mysticism, they platonize. There is nothing original in the edifice."[9] Festugière's study of contemplative theory and practice in Platonism is extensive and original and demonstrates exhaustively the Platonic origins of contemplative practice that subsequently manifested themselves in Christian mysticism.

"The primal god is eternal, ineffable (ἄφατος)," says Albinus.[10] And because this primordial divinity is "ineffable" (ἄφατος), it is only comprehended through the *nous*. The word *nous*, Festugière tells us, is not in his view the same as intellect, if by intellect we mean discursive rationality. Of course, the word "intellection" does exist, so intellect can function actively, just as *nous* can function in the verb *noesis*. And the word "intellect" can encompass more than discursive reason. But *noesis* refers to the "faculty of mystical intuition" whereby we may "enter into contact with [that which] is beyond essence."[11] What we are thereby intuitively united with is not good, bad, or indifferent; neither with nor without qualities; neither accidental nor essential; neither whole nor part; neither moves nor is moved.[12] It can be recognized in "silence" and in the "suppression of all the senses."[13]

One needs to separate from others and from worldly concerns and ascend to the "Transcendent One" by "renouncing all that the mind may conceive," reaching that point at which one is "neither one-self nor someone else," "supremely united by a completely unknowing inactivity of all knowledge," knowing that which is beyond the mind "by knowing nothing."[14] What one knows is not knowledge in the sense of information or conceptual constructs but rather cannot be understood discursively at all: it is direct intuitive knowledge or gnosis that is "beyond every assertion," "beyond every denial," "preëminently simple and absolute," "free of every limitation," and "beyond every limitation."[15]

This absolute transcendence of the One, says Dionysius the Areopagite, "is not in any place, and can neither be seen nor be touched. It is neither perceived nor is it perceptible." It is not "overwhelmed by any earthly passion"; it does not change, divide, decay, or ebb or flow; it is beyond all attributions to it.[16] I cite Dionysius the Areopagite here (the source or headwaters of Christian mysticism), and Albinus and Plotinus earlier, in order to underscore that on this core understanding, the two traditions are in fact exactly the same. Both emphasize the absolute transcendence of the One, and also the fact that it can be perceived, not through discursive conceptual rationality, but through intuitive unity with it. The *nous* within perceives the *nous*.

Now this intuitive recognition of the One is, in the Platonic tradition, referred to with words. We cannot say that the gnosis referred to here is conveyed by language, exactly, but it is possible that the noetic perception can be triggered by the words, even though and perhaps because the words themselves negate all concepts and all sensual and rational attempts to grasp what is being pointed toward by them. Language in this context is inherently paradoxical; it carries its own internal protections against reification or objectification of transcendence as anything conceivable or sensible.

From this point of view, we can see how there is a dialectical or dialogical aspect implicit in the entire Platonic tradition, not only because, of course, Plato himself arranged his writings in the form of dialogues between various characters, but also because the kind of allusive language necessary to refer to transcendence carries an implicit dialogue within it—one is in some sense guided to "triangulate" by the negations and thereby navigate towards the transcendence by knowing what it is not. There is, in other words, one's consciousness, the One, and that which the One is not. By knowing what it is not, one can navigate toward perception of it, and this triangulation can be understood as a kind of internal dialogue. "Behind" the internal dialogue, though, or at its "end," is transcendence of the subject (one's consciousness) and its object (the One). Ultimately, they are the same—*nous.*

Now, what we are considering here is really a metaphysics of literature. Plato's dialogues, Plotinus's *Enneads* (which certainly are also literary), Dionysius the Areopagite's treatises, indeed, the whole of mystical literature, needs to be understood first of all *as* literature, that is, as the symbolic representation on a discursive field of that which transcends discursive consciousness. What is encoded in this literary tradition is not political, social, economic, or any kind of worldly interest, but rather metaphysics in the literal sense of *ta meta ta physika,* (that which is beyond physics and cosmology). While metaphysical truth of the kind being alluded to here cannot be conveyed through literature, it can for certain be alluded to by this kind of encoded language, the most essential instance of which we have just in fact seen.

But the Platonic tradition, particularly in Plotinus's refined development of it, can be understood as an extremely subtle and sophisticated representation of the ascent to transcendent consciousness. The ascent of consciousness is also understandable as theophanic, that is, as the revelation of higher aspects of consciousness arrayed and perceptible as divinities. In Plotinus, these successive revelations correspond to what is sometimes known, rather crudely, as "the three gods," but really the One, the Intellect, and the World-Soul.[17] The World-soul is visible through the harmony of the physical cosmos, which in turn reflects the Thoughts or Ideas of the Intellect, which in turn is transcended by the One that is beyond all things and concepts, unnnameable and purely transcendent. The Intellect is intermediate between transcendence and the physical world, and its divine thoughts are themselves perceivable in our field of consciousness as divinities or gods, each of which is an "opening" into transcendence.

Thus one's movement toward transcendence in the field of consciousness can be represented or understood symbolically in terms of visionary or mystical encounters without this in any way negating the underlying metaphysics of transcendence. Coming to recognize and know deities (theurgy) in this context is how the visionary ascent is representable as literature. Hence theurgic Platonism is not at all a deviation from Platonic metaphysics; it is rather a way of approach to a metaphysics of transcendence through a visionary encounter, and literature itself can also be properly understood in this context, that is, as representations for navigation in the field of consciousness as well as means of self-transcendence.

There is of course a distinction between what we would today term literature and the mystical treatises of Plotinus or of Dionysius the Areopagite. Mystical language in the tradition of Plotinus and Dionysius the Areopagite is not just a "theological" construction, "but a philosophical position taken over directly [by Dionysius] from Neoplatonism." This is true even though, but ultimately because "words are discursive expressions of intellection" and what is beyond all being "transcends all [discursive] knowledge."[18] That is, mystical language in the Platonic tradition points toward what is Real, that is, toward absolute transcendence, but also toward what we might call the relative transcendences of gods or celestial beings. Literature as it is understood in the contemporary secular sense of fiction and poetry largely does no such thing.

So in what ways could we develop a metaphysics of literature, if by literature we mean finely crafted works of secular fiction that entertain and perhaps even elevate readers, but that have no metaphysical orientation, as Platonism itself clearly does? By understanding the Platonic metaphysics that are embedded in its mystical literature, one can develop a reference point on a spectrum along which one can place and through which one can comparatively understand other kinds of literature. At the far end of the spectrum is literature that exemplifies and explicates a Platonic metaphysics, and at the opposite end of the spectrum is literature that exists as a reflection of ordinary or unusual human life without any other purpose than fictional representation, excepting perhaps additional layers of cynicism and/or nihilism. At the one end is literature whose primary, one even may say sole, purpose is to make itself transparent as it explicitly points toward its own transcendence and the transcendence of all linguistic constructions. At the other end is literature that is opaque, that draws attention to itself as literary representation, and that points not beyond itself but back toward ordinary self-other consciousness.

Between these two poles is a spectrum, and by beginning with the Platonic metaphysics of language, we can begin to understand literature more generally in relation to it. But the Platonic metaphysics of language requires us to also understand some essential points about Platonic metaphysics. The first thing to recognize is that the divine or celestial hierarchy is best understood not as a>b>c>d, that is, as a movement from one discrete level to another, at the inception or top of which is the transcendent origin. Rather, as Proclus puts it, "all things are full of gods, and what each has according to nature, it has from there."[19] The gods or henads are the presence of the One as manifested to or in beings, and the transcendent Cause or Origin, the One, is present in all of them at once. To put it another way, summarizes Eric Perl, when Neoplatonic procession as manifestation or unfolding is properly understood, "the supposed opposition between immediate creative presence and mediated production disappears."[20] And the same is true in Dionysius the Areopagite: "[T]here is no opposition, or even distinction, between God's immediate productive presence to all things and the transmission of that presence through the hierarchy of creatures."[21] Perl expresses this as "immediate mediation," meaning that "the archetype" is present "in the image;" all things participate simultaneously in God [the One] "who is Love, Ectasy, Overflow itself."[22] Hence in Dionysian metaphysics, "there is no such thing as an individual a being conceived as a closed, self-contained unit which extrinsically enters into relations with other beings." The principle of reality is "pure Openness or Giving," and thus the being of each is in what it gives to and receives from others through immediate mediation. All beings by nature ecstatically share in divinity through the "communion of intelligences."[23]

The Platonic dialogue can also be understood in this way, with each participant character contributing to and essential to the whole. This is of course true of the classical Platonic dialogues, but it is even true of treatises that may initially appear to be monologues, especially the *Enneads* of Plotinus. Kevin Corrigan observes, in *Reading Plotinus*, that "when one first reads Plotinus, his writings may look like straightforward treatises, even monologues. Before long, however, one becomes aware of an internal dialogue, questioning and answering itself. Other voices enter in major and minor keys, often subliminially, and only such indications as 'and we shall reply to someone who held that view' reveal the presence of hidden interlocutors."[24]

Plotinus's philosophy is, he concludes, "inherently dialectical; it invariably involves a 'we.'" That is, "it is a conversation between friends."[25] And when new voices are heard, sometimes Plotinus incorporates what they have to say into his own thought. This is at heart a metaphysical dialectical process. As Plotinus put it, in coming to know the god, "one must remain within an imprint of him," and when one has recognized that "one is entering into the most blessed thing," one must "give oneself to what is within and become, instead of one who sees, already an object of vision of another who contemplates one shining out with such thoughts as come from there."[26]

In other words—and this is a vital point—literature can be understood as an expression of the same contemplative process that Plotinus is describing, as a discursive representation of visionary encounter wherein *what is known is also the knower*, because both participate in the same inherent reality of the One. This is a central element of Platonic metaphysics, and this metaphysical point, which Perl refers to as "immediate mediation," but which also could be termed "interbeing," is actually a description of an experiential contemplative process, because in the contemplative ascent, as Plotinus tells us directly, the one who contemplates the god begins to realize that that which is contemplated is also contemplating oneself— that the hitherto apparently "solid" barriers between oneself and the imputed other do not exist in the ways one thought they did.

Now I am not suggesting here that all literature operates on the metaphysical level to which Plotinus is referring. But I am suggesting that much of classical literature can be understood *in relation to it*. That is, literature, even secular literature, can be understood as implicitly overcoming the imputed barriers between "us" and "them," because one begins to inhabit the worlds and consciousnesses of others as one reads. Emily Herman, in *The Meaning and Value of Mysticism*, says that "the mystic's desire is fulfilled, not by means of a special organ of spiritual vision, but by the interplay of all the faculties fused into one by the higher Reason.[27] John Scotus Eriugena wrote, "Whoever rises to pure understanding becomes that which he understands. We, while we discuss together, in turn become one another. For if

I understand what you understand, I am become your understanding, and in a certain unspeakable way I am made into you. And also when you entirely understand what I clearly understand, you become my understanding, and from two understandings there arises one."[28]

The metaphysics of Platonism provide the architecture for understanding how literature works, or can work, to join consciousnesses. But there is relatively little precedent for applying this perspective to the study of literature. One author who has made some effort in this direction was Northrop Frye, a major literary critic most well known for his *Anatomy of Criticism* (1957). In this work, Frye observed that "the structural principles of literature are as closely related to mythology and comparative religion as those of painting are to geometry."[29] Frye goes on to develop his analysis of myth in literature by developing a literary typology along a spectrum from religious/mythological in which, particularly in the "apocalyptic" mode, everything is united and fluid, to the naturalistic. Of the world of mythical imagery, he writes, it is "apocalyptic, in the sense of that word already explained, a world of total metaphor, in which everything is potentially identical with everything else, as though it were all inside a single infinite body."[30]

Frye thus presents three main types of literature, moving from

1. The "total metaphorical identification" of "undisplaced myth," which includes two categories, apocalyptic (desirable) and demonic (undesirable). In this "total metaphorical identification," a god can be the sun and a human being all at once. Here, subject and object can be virtually interchangeable.

2. His second type is Romantic—with mythological patterns in a world closer to our own. Myth in Romantic literature operates through "displacement," that is, being linked "in romance by some form of simile: analogy, significant association, incidental accompanying imagery, and the like." Hence in a myth one finds a sun-god or a tree-god; in a romance one finds a man who is associated with the sun symbolically.

3. Frye's third type is "Realism" in quotation marks, which may be more or less bereft of the power of myth, a more or less bare naturalism in which subject observes object,

and in naturalistic modes, "the association [of symbolic imagery] becomes less significant." In its most extreme form, the alienated subject closely describes an alienated object; the isolated individual is trapped in a world of isolated objects, and there is little or no connection between them.[31]

Frye's literary typology fits very neatly into and in effect explicates our larger Platonic metaphysics as it relates to literature. What is more, it is clear from his notebooks that Frye was in fact thinking along these very lines. In one of his late notebooks, he observed that "in the spiritual world everything interpenetrates without violation; nature 'allows of penetration less,' & hence is a constantly aggressive & competitive world. . . . perhaps the spiritual world doesn't know the distinction of full & empty."[32] Or again, "the end of the journey is interpenetration."[33] A "work of literature is a 'creation,' because *the* creation itself is a mirror of consciousness, and, as Rilke says, we are always facing the creation: we can never look out from it as the animals do. The spirit achieves its own . . . apocalyptic new creation through the unconscious inner unification of all its responses."[34] And he observes specifically, "The Buddhists keep saying, with tremendous and unending prolixity, that the subject-object duality is horseshit. Okay, it's horseshit: what's so infernally difficult about that? The fact that it's so difficult to overcome derives from the fact that the metaphorical kernel of subject & object is the contrast of life & death. The person for whom *that's* disappeared really is a sage."[35]

Frye also begins to develop how literature works to overcome subject-object duality. He writes, for instance, that "the myth is neither historical nor anti-historical: it is counter-historical, creating a stasis in the movement of time. The metaphor similarly is counter-logical, creating a stasis in the movement of causality." Hence "the metaphor says 'A is not B' as clearly as it says 'A is B,' and from the point of view of the denial 'A is B' can be only the unit of a purely hypothetical world." And so "*Paradise Lost* is hypothetical in itself, but it's 'real' (whatever that means) to me, not because I share Milton's beliefs but because I possess his metaphors."[36] Thus "imaginative, metaphorical, poetic speech is about the limit with words;" fundamentally, it's "announcing a world beyond speech. This world is first of all an alternation between experiencing as a unit & understanding without words, a larger entity: then it goes beyond that duality."[37]

Frye also considers the realm of archetypes, that is, of the existence of a transcendent realm or realms above this material one. He confides, in one notebook entry, "[F]or a long time I've been preoccupied by the theme of the reality of the spiritual world, including its substantial reality."[38] Thus, just as in Platonism philosophy is a path upward, through the archetypal realm(s) toward transcendence and realization of unity with the One, so too for Frye "the study of literature is one of the paths to self-transformation. That would suggest the possibility of a book on that subject in which Blake himself would have to be a central figure. Rimbaud certainly; de Nerval and Rilke probably, Yeats almost certainly, would bulk very large in a study of the poetic imagination as doing the kind of things that the drug people say drugs do."[39] Frye is suggesting that the study of literature is much more than just a means of diversion, that it can be understood as a spiritual path in its own right, much like Platonic mystical literature.

In a late book, Frye developed and applied his metaphysical typology, taking the title and theme of his work, *The Double Vision* (1991), from William Blake, who in a poem from 1802 observed that "double the vision my eyes do see, / And a double vision is always with me." Frye interprets this poem as meaning that "the conscious subject is not really perceiving until it recognizes itself as part of what it perceives."[40] Later, Frye explains further that "the natural vision of space is founded on the subject-object split," whereas "in the spiritual world everywhere is here, and both a center and a circumference."[41] To see both is Blake's "double vision." Likewise, he continues, there is a natural vision of time (history) and a spiritual vision of time (eternity).[42] And in an extraordinary final passage that seems very close to Plotinus, Frye observes that spirit may "enter a world of higher energies where the separate things spread around objective heres and theres are no longer things to keep bumping into." "In such a spiritual nature," he continues, "no longer the nature of congealed objects, we should be gods or luminous presences ourselves."[43] These are remarkable observations for a literary critic. But Frye was more than that, which is exactly why his work is important.

Not only mystical, but indeed all literature worthy of the name can be understood in terms of the ascent of consciousness. The truth is—and I say this as someone with a PhD in the study of literature, both religious and "secular"—understanding literature in a Platonic context would transform our understanding of it. Currently, in truth we in the academy have little idea why we study literature: there is no longer any prevailing self-understanding. Earlier, there was at least a vague notion of "great books," but even in that case, it was not actually very clear what constituted a great book or what its greatness really did to enoble us, exactly. Frye does not provide the full metaphysical context for understanding literature in terms of the progressive awakening of transcendent states of consciousness, only occasional indications and notes, but he achieved more in this regard than anyone else thus far.

Were we to begin to think about literature in terms of its relation to and effects on how consciousness can move from dualistic to nondualistic through literature, that would create an entirely new and comprehensive way of understanding what literature is for and why and how it works. Of course, that would also upend the way many of us think about poetry and fiction. Needless to say, there is fiction that works primarily to divert us; there are many kinds of fiction and poetry. Frye's typology begins to sort out different levels of literature, however, and I would suggest that the typology would have to be significantly expanded, since in reality it would go from literature of alienation and suffering (extreme dualism) to literature of transcendence accompanied by bliss or transcendence that cannot be described or captured by any concept or description whatever (beyond all dualistic constructs).

Such a model also would take into account the myriad intermediate gradations between these extremes. It is a commonplace that poetry or fiction is inspired, that it comes to one like a gift from beyond. Indeed, I have often thought that what makes us unique as individuals isn't so much our individual ability to create as such but rather our unique capacity to perceive and to convey what exists not only in our own cranium, but also in a realm beyond us to which some have more access than others. The Platonic concept of transcendent ideas, forms, or archetypes and the Platonic concept of the theurgic ascent of consciousness even to the realms where the gods and other transcendent beings dwell have profound significance for how we might understand literature. Of course the details would require—were we to begin to more deeply examine this theme—an entire book of its own. Here let me offer just a few illustrative examples to begin to sketch what I mean.

The first set of authors we might consider is the Romantics. In both British and German Romanticism one finds poets and philosophers whose worldview is in a Platonic lineage, broadly speaking. That is, both groups reflect Platonic themes in their poetry, and in some respects they also convey what we might call a diffused Platonic metaphysics. One author and artist whose work has been explored in this regard is William Blake, of course. In *Blake and Tradition*, Kathleen Raine details the ways that William Blake's art and poetry were indebted to the Platonic tradition; she also discusses this in *Golgonooza, City of Imagination*, and several other works.[44] George Mills Harper also wrote extensively about the visionary poet's indebtedness to the Platonic tradition.[45] Both authors demonstrate that Blake drew from Platonism, in part through the remarkable translations made available by the indefatigable translator Thomas Taylor (1758–1835).[46]

But my point here is not that Blake drew from the Platonic tradition so much as that his extraordinary visual and poetic creativity can be better understood in light of Platonism. That is, Blake's visionary works represent the translation of vision into art. For Blake, the poet is a prophetic intermediary, bringing into the human world what he has seen in the higher spiritual realm that is visible through nature but transcends the natural world. Blake cannot be understood except by recognizing that for him art is both a means of revelation and a means of contemplative ascent. Blake is a theurgic poet.

And indeed the entire Romantic movement arguably can best be understood in a Platonic context. What Wordsworth sees in and through nature is Platonic, which is quite visible when he writes in his Ode on "Intimations of Immortality" that

> There was a time when meadow, grove, and stream,
>   The earth, and every common sight,
>   To me did seem
>   Apparell'd in celestial light,
> The glory and the freshness of a dream.
> It is not now as it hath been of yore;—
>   Turn wheresoe'er I may,
>   By night or day,
> The things which I have seen I now can see no more.

In Wordsworth's famous lines "our birth is but a sleep and a forgetting," when he also refers to "our life's Star," when he observes our soul "cometh from afar / Not in entire forgetfulness, /. . . But trailing clouds of glory do we come," he is without doubt conveying an essentially Platonic worldview (life as "forgetting" and remembering—anamnesis).

But the larger point is that for Blake, for Wordsworth, and to a limited extent for Samuel Taylor Coleridge, to take only these three, their poetry is also a kind of spiritual revelation, just as it is in the twentieth century for the poet Rainer Maria Rilke. For Blake this is obviously so, but it is also so for Wordsworth, and it may even be so for Coleridge, some of whose poetry, notably "Kubla Khan," is so otherworldly in its singular rhythm and beauty that it seems to be translating a realm slightly beyond our time and space to this one. The same may be said of some of the poetry of William Butler Yeats, but it is Rilke who exemplifies what I am referring to, perhaps even as much as does Blake.

Rilke's greatest achievements were the *Duino Elegies* and *The Sonnets to Orpheus*, the latter evoking the ancient Mystery religion, both sublime in their poetic invocations and indications of transcendence. *Duino Elegies* begins with the arresting lines "Wer, wenn ich schriee, hörte mich den aus der Engel / Ordnungen? [Who, when I cry out, hears me among those Angelic Orders?]." Were one of the angels to hold the poet to its heart, he continues, he'd vanish in terror; even their serene scorn is enough to kill us. "Ein jeder Engel ist schrecklich. [Every angel is terrifying]." What makes these lines, and this poem, so powerful is the reader's awareness from the very beginning that what is being described is not only real, but Real. We are being introduced to what is greater than the human and natural worlds, to what is beyond us, above us, and after our short human lives end.

And *The Sonnets to Orpheus* bring the God Orpheus to life in our "inner ear," as the divine singing that awakens the life of nature. We are introduced to the God: "Da stieg ein Baum. O reine Übersteigung./ O Orpheus singt! O hoher Baum im Ohr! / Und alles schwieg. [A tree arises. Oh, pure transcendence / Oh, Orpheus sings! Oh higher tree in the ear! / And all is silent.]." When Orpheus sings, the animals come out of their lairs, freed, because with that call he created temples for them in their "inner hearing." Orpheus, is he "one of us?" Rilke asks. "Nein, aus beiden / Reichen erwuchs seine weite Natur. [No, out of both / realms grows his wide nature.]." Here again we are drawn into a vast cosmos, one in which the God exists in a mysterious and profound way beyond what we can fully grasp. Orpheus belongs to "both realms," to that of the Gods, but also to that of nature, and human beings can be the medium through which he moves between those two realms.

Rilke's poetry is powerful and moving precisely because it conveys so well this communication and movement of consciousness between realms, as well as a sense of the power and inconceivable vastness of the beings beyond us, call them angels or gods. For Rilke, eternity is not just a word but a reality into which one can go and come back, timelessness that is present to us now. More than that of any other poet, Rilke's poetry is vatic, Orphic, a portal into a world where we leave behind materialism, naturalism—and suddenly what once may have been for us only distant concepts (the ancients' view of the dead as shades; the power of the god; the pregnant silence of eternity) through Rilke's poetic genius become alive, present, authentic for us.

Another author whose work clearly derived from her "translation" from other realms is Ithell Colquhoun (1906–1988). Colquhoun was a surrealist painter, a poet, a novelist, and a practitioner of magic whose novels *Goose of Hermogenes* and *I Saw Water* also exemplify in a different way what I am referring to here.[47] Colquhoun said that her novels, in particular, *I Saw Water*, came to her in dreams, that the imagery and narrative in the books was presented in stages through dreams, and that the process of writing was to be faithful to the larger dream narrative that was being revealed to her. There are other examples of revealed works of art—W. B. Yeats's *A Vision* comes to mind—but Colquhoun is unusual in that she made it clear that her novels are not just "her" creative production, but come from somewhere else and reveal somewhere else, a reality beyond the quotidian world.

In this regard, we might note the plots of both of Colquhoun's novels. *Goose of Hermogenes* is about a narrator who journeys to an island presided over by her uncle, a singular man. The island, we discover, may be an island of the dead, just as *I Saw Water* is set on an island of the dead named Menec, which is actually the name of a vast array of standing stones in Carnac, in Breton, France, along the coast. In *Goose of Hermogenes*, the narrator tells us, "I am dead, it is only my unhappy ghost that wanders through my Uncle's mansion and demesne."[48] Colquhoun's novels, particularly *Goose of Hermogenes*, incorporate all manner of mysterious alchemical and occult symbols, ideas, and themes, so much so that often two pages bear rereading half a dozen or more times to draw out the richness of the allusions. And in both, a narrator, presumably dead, goes to the island of the dead and there undergoes a spiritual process of transmutation.

Colquhoun's novels are haunting and fantastic because they incorporate, far more than most fiction, elements from beyond what can be seen with the eyes and grasped with the hands; for Colquhoun, the other world, a world of the dead and a world in which we can be transmuted, is present and both invoked and conveyed in her fiction and art. I am offering her work as exemplifying a kind of literary art that cannot be understood at all except by recognizing that this is a world where the boundaries between self and other, us and nature and the land of the dead, the places of the gods, are permeable, interwoven with one another. Here, there is no clear subject looking at an object, but rather we are introduced to an occult world—*occult*—where what is ordinarily visible is hidden, and what is ordinarily invisible is now visible. It is not a literature of transcendence; it is a literature of what is hidden, of the twilight world where different realms meet. In Frye's typology, it is an unabashedly mythical world.

As Frye himself suggested, an artist who clearly began to develop in prose a nondualistic understanding of literature was William Butler Yeats. Early in his *Essays* (1924), Yeats included an extended reflection entitled "Magic," which he begins by observing that "the borders of our mind are ever shifting, and . . . many minds can flow into one another, as it were, and create or reveal a single mind, a single energy."[49] The essay as a whole includes many instances from Yeats's own experience of people sharing dreams, visions, symbols, or images across the seeming barriers of time and space. He reflects that the origin of poetry and music is in magic, just as the "musician or poet enchants and charms and binds with a spell his own mind when he would enchant the mind of others." The authentic artist is one whose "seeming transitory mind" is "made out of many minds," acting as a vehicle even for "the genius of the tribe" or "of the world."[50] Yeats's understanding of literature is infused with his recognition that literature is based in the transcendence of self and other.

Hence, when Yeats turns his attention to the great poet Shelley, his admiration leads him to reflect on Shelley's philosophy of mind and on how for Shelley, mind's great symbol is water, in particular, water flowing through dark caverns.[51] This symbolism of water and caverns, Yeats traces back to Blake and from Blake to the Neoplatonic philosopher Porphyry. "Again and again one finds some passing allusion to the cave of man's mind, or to the caves of his youth, or to the cave of mysteries we enter at death, for to Shelley as to Porphyry it is more than an image of life in the world."[52] Yeats thought that Shelley might have followed these inward images "into that far household, where the undying gods await all whose souls have become as simple as flame," but alas, "he was born in a day when the old wisdom had vanished, and was content merely to write verses, and often with little thought of more than verses."[53] In other words, Shelley was not really in touch with the deeper and transcendent dimensions from which his own work emerged. For Yeats, it is not enough to be great at creating verses. Poetry, for him, springs from deep and shared sources, and greatness requires philosophical awareness of those sources and of one's own fidelity to them.

My purpose here is not to offer a catalogue or survey of authors who exemplify a nondualistic understanding, but rather to indicate authors whose work either implicitly or explicitly demonstrates the larger point here—that our understanding of literature can be illuminated by what I am terming a metaphysics of literature. And as it happens, Platonic mysticism provides us with exactly that. What is more, Platonism is a natural reference point for and influence in the Western literary tradition, sometimes explicit, often implicit. Emblematic of both is Ralph Waldo Emerson's work—his essays often reference Platonism directly, but as I showed in *American Gurus*, Platonism also infuses much of his work beneath the surface, visible only when one knows the sources from which he is drawing.[54]

I mention these authors, not because they are the same or because they exemplify mystical literature as such—they don't—but because their works are only comprehensible in a larger, nonmaterialistic context. And that larger context, the one to which they belong, is fundamentally Platonic. Their works can be understood best by reference to Platonic metaphysics, according to which there is an ascending or celestial hierarchy, at the apex of which is the complete transcendence of subject and object. Their work is not devoted to unveiling that complete transcendence, the ultimate ground of all things, but rather to communication with the hidden aspects of our world, with the gods, with the archetypal realms, with spirits. Their poems and narratives open up glimpses of timelessness in and beyond nature.

One key to understanding literature in new ways is through what Dionysius the Areopagite called the *via positiva*, that is, the way through images. In his treatise on this subject, Dionysius discusses how one may come to the divine through similes and analogies, but sometimes metaphors function best by being unlike that toward which they are pointing. In *The Divine Names*, Dionysius describes how one can ascend through "acts of heavenly contemplation"[55] of images and names of the divine, and in *The Celestial Hierarchy*, he observes further that "everything, then, can be a support for contemplation," and even "dissimilar similarities" can reveal beings "which are both intelligible and intelligent."[56] It is a great pity we do not possess Dionysius's lost treatise *The Symbolic Theology*, for that would no doubt provide us with even more clues as to how to develop a science of literature as a map of and set of keys to different aspects of consciousness.

The ways we think of literature are often too limited, no doubt largely as a result of prevailing worldviews that obscure what poets and writers of fiction, particularly romantic fantasy, can offer us. Literature can enchant us, open us to what is higher than our mundane consciousness, give us entrée into realms ordinarily hidden from us. But *how* can it do this? What are the means by which Rilke enchants us with the songs of Orpheus? The science of consciousness must include the science of literature, that is, the study of how literature can open us to the more profound dimensions of our world, of ourselves, and of what lies beyond both. Of course, the most profound literature of all is mystical literature that points directly toward the ultimate ground, and it is to that most transcendent of subjects that we now turn.

CHAPTER SIX

Transcendence

By early in the twenty-first century, it had become something of a commonplace in the humanities that we had entered not just a "postmodern," but what's more, a "postmetaphysical" age. As some scholars put it, "current academic thinking on religion displays an intense skepticism toward any metaphysical referent or transcendental signifier in religious discourse."[1] The underlying notion is a declaration that "the 'transcendent'" (in quotation marks) gods or spirits only exist as "discursive entities," that "religious truth" has no ontological status and is only a discursive product.[2] While some scholars championed a "bracketing" of metaphysical "truth claims" in the interest of remaining "objective," increasingly others subscribed to a neo-Kantian skepticism, asserting dogmatically, as Mark C. Taylor put it, "Consciousness . . . deals only with signs and never reaches the thing in itself." Thus "there is no logos to be revealed, no secret to be uncovered, no truth to be discovered."[3] But on what, exactly, are such confident assertions based?

Across the gamut of "postmetaphysical" and antimetaphysical works, what we find is that they are consistently based on only one thing: an assertion by discursive rational consciousness that it alone exists and has validity. In other words, the foundation for all of the myriad assertions that mysticism is a discursive cultural-linguistic product without any "real" metaphysical referent that we ourselves can experience, for the neo-Kantian skepticism that we can never know anything more than our own discursive type of consciousness, for the claims of deconstructionist and postmodernist authors of the late twentieth century, for the trumpeted death of metanarratives—

all of that is based on just saying so. In other words, ironically, the attempted dismissal of metaphysical truth claims as a "discursive product" is itself actually only—*only*—a discursive product. It is, in the end, a confidence game.

It is really quite interesting how the contemporary chorus, dismissing "essentialism" and rejecting Platonic mysticism more broadly, developed between the midtwentieth and early twenty-first centuries, because it is actually based in nothing other than the choice to join the chorus itself. That is, while there are some vitriolic denunciations of perennialism, mysticism, and Platonism, those are not based on the refutation of Platonism or Platonic mysticism, but rather on its rejection as unacceptably intuitionistic, or insufficiently materialistic, "naïve," "irrational," or some other label along those lines.[4] Often this rejection of Platonism comes from a Marxist-derived rejection of religion more generally and from a concomitant assertion of the primacy of economics, materiality, society, physicality, and so forth. And it is almost always also based on a misunderstanding or misinterpretation of Platonism as dualistic, protototalitarian, and the like.

But there is another perspective, one that seems insufficiently articulated today, elements of which as we have seen were more or less taken for granted in the nineteenth and even into the early twentieth centuries by most scholars of mysticism, and indeed, still is broadly understood by many scholars of Christian mysticism. This perspective is based squarely in the tradition of Platonic mysticism that runs from Plato and Plotinus through Neoplatonism into Christianity via Dionysius the Areopagite, John Scotus Eriugena, and Meister Eckhart.

Many of the interpretive problems in the study of mysticism dissolve of their own accord if one understands this metaphysical perspective clearly. And since it is the perspective of Platonic mysticism itself, it hardly makes sense to attempt to unilaterally dismiss it or assert that it is wrong because we modern sophisticates deem it so. It makes more sense to seek to understand it and its implications on its own terms first of all. Hence, for instance, there has been some scholarly controversy over how exactly we are to understand the veridicality of mystical treatises.[5] And to avoid a perennialist or Platonic perspective, scholars develop a whole array of complicated solutions.[6] But there is a different and more straightforward resolution: first, by understanding overarching Platonic metaphysics, and second, by recognizing that we are looking at the records of contemplative insights within that metaphysical context.

It is important to recognize that the tradition of Platonic mysticism is not dualistic, as it is often claimed to be. The alleged dualism often is derived from a misunderstanding concerning the Platonic "realm of Forms" or "realm of Ideas." It is often depicted as separate from and opposed to the physical world, thus representing the kind of matter/spirit dualism often also alleged of the Gnostics of late antiquity. It is probable that Platonism, Gnosticism, and Hermetism are all variants on a theme, but in any case, of Platonism one can say for certain that it is not dualistic because in Pythagorean-Platonic tradition the Ideas or Forms are the archetypal patterns that inform the natural world. The contemplative ascent in this tradition can be understood as a movement inward toward comprehending the divine powers and patterns that manifest outwardly in the natural world, but are themselves also beyond it.

Some contemporary scholars of mysticism describe mystical experience in dualistic terms even when describing what is termed nondualistic. Robert K. C. Forman refers to a "dualistic mystical state (DMS)" in which one experiences an enduring separate "witness" aspect of consciousness.[7] Likewise, in *The Serpent's Gift*, Jeffrey Kripal refers to mysticism as represented by a doubled mode of consciousness.[8] Both of these scholars are strongly influenced by Hinduism and in particular the idea of the transcendent Self or Atman that is ultimately identical to Brahman. But Platonic tradition is closer to Mahayana or Vajrayana Buddhism and does not privilege a separate "witness" consciousness.

In the tradition of Platonic mysticism, the soul is said to recognize in intellection the ground of truth that is not other than itself. Plotinus says that "when the soul wishes to see [the One] by itself, it is just by being with it that it sees, and by being one with it that it is one, and it is not capable of thinking that it possesses what it seeks, because it is not other than that which is being known."[9] On this passage Sara Rappe comments that it describes the moment when the soul, accustomed to discursive rationality, comes to a realization that leads it "outside the strictures of discursive thought."[10]

It is important to continue here for a moment. In this supremely rich contemplative passage from Plotinus, we do not see a "witness" consciousness that perceives eternity alongside rational consciousness. Rather, Rappe points out, in this passage, "the initial locus of awareness referred to in the text (the soul) is displaced by another kind of consciousness," which "could only be called pristine awareness, immediacy of apprehension, or even self-authorizing consciousness."[11] Commenting on *Enneads* 1.4, Rappe explains that in this process of realization, "the mind comes to be aware of an activity that is 'before awareness,' and it does this by 'turning thought back on itself,' and even that comes about quite naturally when the [discursive] mind's productions come to a halt, leaving it finally 'in peace.' "[12] In other words, "the discursive mind in setting aside its discursive activity becomes transparent," in a "direct awareness of awareness that coincides with a freedom from attachment to particular thoughts." This, she continues, is "objectless knowing that characterizes intellect."[13]

I have drawn so extensively on Rappe's commentary on Plotinus here because she captures perhaps better than anyone else the contemplative process that Plotinus is describing. It is quite difficult to do justice to Plotinus's subtlety of language as he seeks to describe the contemplative experience in which the mind perceives its own nature. The process of contemplative observation is one in which the observing awareness, by observing attentively, is through that very process become transparent and thus is transmuted from discursive awareness to a nondiscursive awareness. This process is not dualistic, nor is it nondualistic—it cannot be adequately captured in linguistic conceptual terms, but only can be referred to, because it is clearly in Plotinus's work a process that one must experience for oneself. His prose represents as careful a guide for this inner contemplative process as he can present.

What we are discussing here is not unique to Plotinus, but is in fact there in Plato's dialogues and letters as well. In *The Origins of the Christian Mystical Tradition*, Andrew Louth points out that in Plato's *Symposium*, the Good is "the Sun of the intelligible realm," and "in a sense, *beyond* knowledge and truth."[14] Louth goes on to observe, "The unknowability of the ultimately Real, the source of all reality, and the state of ecstasy that comes upon the soul as it comes into the presence of the ultimately Real clearly go together. The Form of the Good is unknowable, and so, if the soul is to know it, it must in that act of knowing break through the normal limits of knowledge."[15] Indeed, Plato in his *Seventh Letter* says of the ultimate knowledge that is the goal of philosophy, "it does not admit at all of verbal expression like other studies," but rather through communion with it "it is brought to birth in the soul. . . . like light kindled by a leaping spark, and thereafter it nourishes itself."[16] This is the *theoria* of that which is beyond knowledge.

The French scholar André-Jean Festugière, in his classic work on contemplation in the Platonic tradition, wrote very much along the same lines. He observed that "the One or the Good is in truth ineffable. One touches it, one is united with it by *theoria*, but one cannot define it." He said, "It transcends all essences, being the principle that determines them as essence."[17] The master guides the disciple towards the contemplative act but cannot produce or communicate it, because the contemplative experience is lived by the individual. This contemplative realization does not belong to the realm of knowledge because it is beyond the division of subject and object.

One finds this exact Platonic contemplative tradition carried into Christianity through Dionysius the Areopagite, and from him, in turn, many others, among them John Scotus Eriugena. Elsewhere we have already looked closely at Dionysius's *Mystical Theology*, so here we will instead draw on Eriugena, who referred to the transcendent reality as a kind of *nihil* or nothingness. Eriugena writes that the divine goodness is "ineffable, incomprehensible, and inaccessible"; it is "unknown to all intellects, whether human or angelic, because it is superessential and supernatural." He adds that "in no existing thing is it understood, since it is beyond all things." When it is understood as incomprehensible on account of its excellence, it is not improperly called 'nothing.' "[18] This is experienced "by a certain ineffable descent into the things that are," in which it is "beheld by the mind's eye," where "it alone is found to be in all things, and it is and was and shall be." What is more, in its transcendence it is "nothing," but "in its theophanies it is said to proceed, as it were, out of nothing into something."[19] But this is "secretly" understood.

What we can trace, in other words, is a continuous tradition of Platonic mysticism according to which there is an ineffable and indescribable transcendent ground beyond all phenomena, and further, that all phenomena ceaselessly emerge theophanically out of this ground. Eriugena says that "the Divine Goodness which is called 'Nothing' for the reason that, beyond all things that are and that are not, it is found in no essence, descends from the negation of all essences into the affirmation of the essence of the whole universe," "from formlessness into innumerable forms and species."[20] In other words, this transcendent ground is inherent in all phenomena. It is the primordial ground.

Buddhism developed far beyond the Platonic tradition in this regard, but one could say that the Platonic tradition did have at its center a recognition of transcendence of subject and object; that much is clear not only from a close reading of the original texts but also from the illuminating commentary of the most perceptive recent and contemporary scholars. In Buddhist tradition, there are two aspects of mind training. The first is *shamatha*, which means to stabilize and quiet the mind, and the second is *vipashyana*, or insight. Tulku Urgyen put it this way: "According to ordinary shamatha and vipashyana, shamatha is first cultivated and then vipashyana is pursued. Cultivating shamatha means to produce a state of mental stillness and then to train in it. Pursuing or seeking the insight of vipashyana means trying to identify what it is that remains quiet. . . . The true and authentic vipashyana is the empty and cognizant nature of mind."[21]

In vipashyana or insight, the mind looks at its own nature. The *Ratnakūta Sutra* includes the following dialogue:

> Thereupon the incarnate monk spoke: O venerable ones, concerning the mind which is formless, undemonstrable, without appearance, intangible, groundless, and invisible, can it be conceived as dwelling inside, outside, or in between?

> The monks replied: No sir, this is not so.

> The incarnate monk asked: Venerable ones, if the mind is formless, undemonstrable, without appearance, intangible, groundless, and invisible, then there is nothing to observe inside, outside, or in between. Do you suppose that it has not evolved as a perfect reality?

> They replied: No sir, this is not so.

> He who searches for the mind cannot find it inside or outside of himself, or both outside and inside. He can neither find it in his psychophysical aggregates, in the elemental realms, nor in the sense faculties. Then, because he cannot find the mind, he explores inwardly the stream of his mind with the assumption that a thought arises from a perceptive image. He contemplates whether a perceptive image and mind exist distinctly from one and another or whether they are identical. If the image is separate from

the mind, then there are two kinds of mind. If the image
is the mind itself, then how can the mind "see" the mind,
because the mind cannot 'see' the mind itself.[22]

Likewise in Mahayana Buddhism, the *Prajnaparamita Sutra* famously
emphasizes that "form is emptiness, emptiness is form" and that in
emptiness there is "no form, no sensation, no perception, no volition,
no consciousness, no seeing, no hearing, no smelling, no tasting, no
touching, no body, no mind."

And in Vajrayana Buddhism, transcendence is sometimes referred
to as "primordial consciousness" that is identical with the "absolute
space" (*dharmadhatu*). Alan Wallace puts it this way: "The realization
of absolute space by primordial consciousness transcends all distinctions of subject and object, mind and matter, indeed, all words and
concepts. Such insight does not entail the meeting of a subjective
mode of consciousness with an objective space, but rather the nondual realization of the intrinsic *unity* of absolute space and primordial consciousness."[23] Wallace distinguishes clearly between what he
terms the "substrate" consciousness that is "the relative ground of
the mind," perceived through the cultivation of *shamatha* (calming
of the mind) meditation, and "the absolute space of phenomena
[that] can be realized only through the cultivation of contemplative
insight (*vipashyana*)."[24]

The Buddhist tradition is so vast, and so detailed, with so many
practitioners and treatises developed over millennia, that it provides
far more documentation concerning aspects of consciousness than any
other tradition, including Platonism. But there remains an underlying
and obvious question. Given that the essential truth of Buddhism is
anatman (no-self) and *sunyata* (emptiness), one has to ask whether
what is being described in the tradition of Platonic mysticism, especially the apophatic transcendence emphasized by Plotinus, Damascius, Dionysius the Areopagite, John Scotus Eriugena, and Meister
Eckhart, is insight into the fundamental ground out of which active
mental processes emerge (the substrate consciousness or *bhavanga*.[25]
Indeed, Wallace remarks that the recognition of the ground state of
consciousness is found not only in Buddhist but also in non-Buddhist
contemplative traditions.[26]

In the contemporary academic world, as we have seen, this
idea that contemplative practices can guide us to the same realization is non grata—all kinds of objections are raised against it. It is

perilously close to the perennial philosophy, which is as we have seen largely out of favor. But when we begin to recognize that in this field of inquiry direct contemplative experience (empirical research) is necessary in order to confirm it directly for oneself, then one has to begin to wonder about whether the tradition of Platonic mysticism, whose core descriptions are so akin to those in Buddhism, is exploring the same terrain that Buddhism has far more exhaustively catalogued and investigated.

That they are fundamentally the same was the conclusion reached by the Roman Catholic monk Willigis Jäger, who after years practicing in a Zen Buddhist monastery in Japan, came back to Europe as a recognized Zen teacher and began to explore and then teach also in the tradition that I here am calling Platonic mysticism. We looked earlier at Jäger and his personal and bibliographical history, so I will not rehearse that here. What I will do is focus on Jäger's observations concerning what he regards as the essential mystical experience, the opening of higher transpersonal consciousness, which in Zen is called *kensho*. Jäger writes as an erudite reader and as a practitioner both of Zen Buddhism and of Western mysticism.

As a practitioner and a scholar, Jäger observes that "the mystical level of consciousness is transpersonal. On that level, there is no longer an ego that asserts itself as an independent subject in dualistic opposition to an objective world."[27] But "anyone who denies that there is such a level of consciousness has already blocked the way to mysticism at the outset. It won't be possible to convince such a person with logical arguments. Mysticism is not a matter of faith, but of experience."[28] Jäger continues "anyone who has had a deep mystical experience has realized the one and true essence," and "the One is experienced and, according to the individual person, expressed in an unmistakeable way."[29]

Asked what the signs of such an experience are, Jäger replies that in it "emptiness" is also "fullness." This profound experience is

> the fullness pregnant with myriad possibilities. It contains all capabilities and is both origin and creation. It is coming home to our original home where nothing is lacking: Laughing but not laughing about something, just laughing; happy, but not happy about something; limitless love, but no "I love you." Paradoxically, there is neither love nor hate here, neither life nor death, neither you nor me, no

boundaries, no space, no time. *It* walks along with lightness, matter-of-factness, and freedom. All polarity is gone. Nothing is absurd; on the contrary, everything is fully natural. . . . Even thoughts bubble up out of nowhere and disappear. It is my experience, but this experience shows itself in everything that I am saying here or have ever written. That's why my words often sound unusual. That's why they are also hard to understand from time to time. They come from another level of experience.[30]

Jäger remarks that "anyone can have such an experience unexpectedly and with no prior preparation," as did "Rilke," for example, but it is possible also through practice to stabilize oneself in this transpersonal consciousness that Jäger describes in the passage above. Again mysticism, or "transconfessional spirituality" "does not mean a religion beyond religions, but rather a *religiosity* beyond religions. And this religiosity is a basic element of our human nature." It is "part of our own nature on a very deep level, to open ourselves to wholeness and oneness."[31] The significance of Jesus and Buddha is "the reached[,] what we as human beings are capable [of] reaching: they experienced the primary reality and endeavored to convey that experience to others by showing them how they could come to the same realization."[32]

Jäger focuses on what he terms "the experience of the Primary Reality, my name for 'the One and the True."[33] In this experience, "there are no longer any religions to be united, as there is no differentiation in that reality."[34] From this perspective, different religions like Christianity and Buddhism are like "stained-glass windows" that give a particular hue or shape to the light, but "the actual fact is the light."[35] This light is "the naked present." "Anyone who actually breaks through into this other dimension breaks through to timelessness, or we could say into the present moment . . . timelessness . . . the primary reality."[36] This primary reality is our true nature, not the ego, and in that sense, "mysticism is no less than the search for our true identity."[37]

I have detailed Jäger's view here because he represents someone with a broad and deep knowledge of the full Western tradition the way we have been considering it here, that is, from the pre-Socratic and Platonic traditions through Dionysius the Areopagite and into Christian mysticism. He incorporates those traditions directly into

his exposition in a natural way, effortlessly drawing on them, referring to the *philosophia perennis* and emphasizing what he terms "the
primary reality," which he uses synonymously with the Platonic terms
"the One" and "the truth," as well as Christian-inflected terms like
"divine being."

But there are other scholars who also have a deep familiarity
with the Western Christian tradition, or the Western and Eastern
traditions, as the case may be, and also are themselves contemplative practitioners or guides for others. Among the most prominent
of those is Martin Laird, who has published two books introducing
Christian contemplative practice to the general reader, *Into the Silent
Land: A Guide to the Christian Practice of Contemplation* (2006), and
A Sunlit Absence: Silence, Awareness, and Contemplation (2011). Like
Jäger, Laird is in the Roman Catholic tradition, in Laird's case as an
Augustinian clergy member and professor at Villanova University, as
well as a teacher of contemplative prayer. His books engage scholarly
sources but center on contemplative practice.

Laird does not emphasize the Platonic dimension of Christian
mysticism—his sources are primarily from the Desert Fathers, the
Eastern Orthodox or hesychastic tradition, Augustine, and various
Christian mystics. He does draw from Plotinus, Dionysius the Areopagite, and *The Cloud of Unknowing*, however, primarily not in terms
of sheer transcendence, but more in terms of specific avuncular advice
about contemplative practice. Laird's books are primers, meant for a
general audience, and focused on the practical dimensions of inner
life, how to realize that we are not the same as the "video" that plays
in our head, that there is a deeper and silent realm of consciousness,
while beyond that is the "sunlit absence" of the "ungraspable" stable
inner awareness of "inner light."[38]

Laird puts it this way in *A Sunlit Absence*: there is an inner awakening to a "Vastness" that is aware. He quotes St. Diadochos, who
counsels, "You should not doubt that the intellect, when it begins
to be strongly energized by the divine light, becomes so completely
translucent that it sees its own light vividly." He then writes,

> To the conceptual mind this awakening differs from pre-
> vious ones. This luminous, flowing Vastness is constantly
> present whether we turn our gaze within or without, for
> in this Vastness there is no within versus without. This
> ground-awareness does not joust with divine presence-

> versus-absence, for it embraces both. . . . Untouched by
> time, but without being excluded by time, it is yet within
> time but without being contained by time.[39]

Awareness, he continues, is not aware *of* something, but rather is more like "aware-ing," for "by virtue of its simplicity it grounds all things and therefore is never separate from anything."[40]

Now there are two aspects to what Laird writes here. First, of course, is that it has the unmistakable ring of direct experience in contemplative practice. He is describing contemplative experience, seeking to put into words his own contemplative observation just as did Plotinus so many centuries before. Second, the Western dimension of Laird's work (and to be sure there is a hesychastic Eastern dimension as well) is clearly in the current of Platonic mysticism we have been charting here. That is, his references include those who transmitted this current into and through Christianity: Dionysius (Denys) the Areopagite, Meister Eckhart, *The Cloud of Unknowing*, and *The Book of Privy Counsel*, to list just those sources that are woven through Laird's books. Plato himself and the Neoplatonic tradition as such are not visible here, but through these sources, and as an essential part of the tradition Laird represents, they are there nonetheless.

But let us step back and consider this subject from another vantage point. What we have been looking at are assertions, from numerous sources, that it is possible for us as human beings to be aware in a way that transcends subject and object and that also is imbued with what is variously described as impartial compassion or love. That there are different degrees of such awareness, that there are greater or lesser degrees of depth as charted in great detail in Buddhism, is another matter. What we are considering here is a fundamental assertion that there is a kind of awareness that is accessible to us as human beings, which can be termed "primal ground," "primordial ground," or "transcendence."

The descriptions of the awakening of this kind of awareness are virtually identical in Platonic mysticism from antiquity to the present day (as exemplified also in the contemporary contemplative teachers Willigis Jäger and Martin Laird) and similar to those in the Buddhist texts and exemplars we quoted, including B. Alan Wallace, himself a scholar and contemporary Buddhist teacher of meditation. This is not to say that these traditions are identical—I am not claiming that they are—but rather that they are both *pointing toward* the results of contemplative practice that transcend any particular tradition because the state of awareness engaged is itself beyond subject and object or mental constructs.

There is, in other words, in this transcendence of subject and object also a metaphysical reference point—sometimes referred to as the still point at the center of the wheel—that is the center of the tradition of Platonic mysticism in light of which the other elements of that tradition can be understood. That in turn leads us inexorably to the question as to whether what we are considering here under the name "transcendence," or "primordial ground," is in fact a *human* experience, one that by its very nature cannot belong to any tradition as such, but rather that traditions can point toward, guide toward it.

Here we might return to the concluding reflections of an early twentieth-century scholar of mysticism who wrote, "[T]here is a Gnosis," which "is the life blood of religion." and, "In the Mysticism of the future the speculative and the intuitive elements must once more interact, as they did in the greatest Mysticism of the past," for "the fire still burns on the altars of Plotinus."[41] Certainly it is true that if what is understood by these many figures is, as they all say, beyond the confines of time and space even while also within those confines, beyond all opposites and all conceptual constructs, then it is not only something belonging to our past but also to our present and our future. The next chapter will consider the present and future possibilities offered by the study of mysticism or, rather, as we may better term it, contemplative science.

CHAPTER SEVEN

Contemplative Art,
Contemplative Science

At heart, the Platonic tradition belongs to both art and science. From the very beginning, Plato's dialogues were artistic, theatrical, and literary, as well as philosophical creations, conveying multiple meanings through parables and allusions. But there is another way of understanding this tradition, one that might seem at odds with the artistic aspects of Platonism, but that is just as present. I refer to Platonic mysticism as contemplative science. These two aspects of the Platonic tradition, far from being at odds with one another, in fact form a complementary whole, for Platonic mysticism can be understood both as contemplative art and as contemplative science.

The artistic dimension of the Platonic tradition is deeply woven into it from the very beginning. It is certainly present in the dialogues themselves, theatrical creations of literary and philosophical artifice whose memorable characters express different aspects of ancient Greek thought in engaging exchanges. And the characters are full and mysterious. Who is Socrates? What is he? Today, as a thousand years ago, and a thousand years from now, people can ask such questions because the figure of Socrates looms larger than life over the whole of the dialogues as provocateur, jester, initiator, mystagogue, shaman, poet, and philosopher all at once.

And the Platonic tradition indisputably is a wellspring of artistic inspiration, as we see during the Italian Renaissance in particular. Marsilio Ficino's translations made available core works of the Platonic and Hermetic tradition and provided a metaphysical context for understanding art. This metaphysical context is vital; it is what allows us to understand art as more than simply hedonic, for art conceived in and reflecting this larger metaphysics provides a passage from aesthetics to transcendence by way of beauty. Of particular importance for understanding art as a means of passage from beauty to Beauty is the work of Plotinus. What makes the Italian Renaissance particularly important is that Platonic aesthetics is there directly reflected in artistic works of the time.

First, we should sketch a bit the Plotinian understanding of art and beauty. For Plotinus, a beautiful work of art is not merely a collection of material parts organized in a pleasing manner; it rather manifests the harmony of intellectual and transcendent beauty. The artist realizes this beauty in the work of art, and the viewer also realizes it: the work of art is truly a medium or means for perceiving what is beyond it, but nonetheless manifested in it. To perceive beauty in a work of art—Botticelli's *Birth of Venus*, for example—is mystical in the sense that one in a mysterious way unites with that image by recognizing the pleasure of perceiving its beauty, which simultaneously is the perception of transcendent beauty.

We see this in Botticelli's masterpiece *The Birth of Venus*, where the nude image of Venus on the seashell exemplifies *nuditas virtualis*, the nudity of virtue and the state of innocence. Here nudity reveals the purity of the perfect human form resplendent with divine virtue. But it is more than seeing what is beautiful, for the Plotinian understanding is that in order to see what is beautiful, one must become what is beautiful. Plotinus observed in his treatise on beauty, "No eye ever saw the sun without becoming beautiful. You must first become all godlike and beautiful if you intend to see God and beauty."[1] This perception of beauty is itself virtuous, and nudity embodies its purity.

We see this understanding of *nuditas virtualis* reflected in ancient Greek and Roman classical art, especially statuary, and it reappears again in the Italian Renaissance in the works of many artists of the period, including Sandro Botticelli, of course, but also Michelangelo, Giorgio Vasari, Leon Battista Alberti, and others.[2] The male nudes of Michelangelo, although they have solidity and detail of musculature and form, like the ancient Greek statuary in their purity of form also represent (as does Botticelli's Venus) "universal beauty" as manifested "through a simple, flowing, harmonious form." "The beauty of the figures' lines," their "aloof" faces, "mean[s] that they possess an "ethereal, mysterious existence," as one critic beautifully put it.[3]

The perception of beauty in these figures is a contemplative act. As Plotinus put it, when the soul ascends to the realm of intellect, it realizes that there one sees transcendent beauty, the beauty of the essences or transcendent ideas. The work of contemplative art becomes a portal through which we glimpse something of the intelligible world that is itself at once good, true, and beautiful because it cannot be otherwise.[4] One has to awaken one's inner sight, Plotinus tells us, and he gives us instruction on how to do this. We need to see ourselves as beautiful, he says, and to achieve this we must like the creator of a statue chip away what is not beautiful until you have become "nothing but true light, not measured by dimensions," "unmeasured," "superior to all quantity," and "when you have become this, then you have become sight," and "this alone is the eye that sees the great beauty."[5]

Of course, passages like these sound mystical because in fact they *are* mystical; they reflect Platonic mysticism in practice. And Platonic mysticism in this context can be said to have two aspects—art and science—but Platonic contemplative art only at first appears to be a different subject than contemplative science. In reality, both must be understood within the larger context of the Platonic metaphysics that inform them. A work of classical contemplative art, be it statuary or painting, is not created at random but reflects a classical canon of proportion and harmony incorporating geometrical patterns. And that canon in turn reflects the ancient Pythagorean-Platonic tradition that recognizes how geometric and mathematical harmony is inherent in the cosmos. Beauty, in this tradition, is pleasing because it reveals harmonic perfection that is inherent both in ideal nature and in the ideal human form.

From a Platonic perspective, when we see beauty in art, or in nature, we are also seeing the transcendent beauty that inheres in what we see. By our perceiving it, we not only recognize it but beyond that in some sense unite with it through the act of perception. For an artist who is imbued with the classical understanding of art by training as well as by direct observation and familiarity, what I am terming here Platonic metaphysics is background. That is, the artist may have had access to Marsilio Ficino's translation of Plotinus, or of Dionysius the Areopagite, for instance, the *Celestial Hierarchy*.

But such access is not necessary for the artist to absorb through classical art itself the metaphysics embodied in it.

I would argue that one also finds Platonic metaphysics in the greatest paintings of the nineteenth century, in particular those of the American Hudson River School. Now it is true, as I've shown elsewhere, that the literature of American Transcendentalism, especially the essays and poetry of Ralph Waldo Emerson, but also the work of his friend Bronson Alcott, is deeply imbued with Platonism.[6] Certainly Emerson's works were well known in the middle and late nineteenth century, so some influence is undoubtedly possible, indeed, probable. But many of the works of the magnificent paintings in this school lend themselves to a Platonic explication.

One of the greatest of these painters was Frederic Edwin Church (1826–1900), whose best modern critic was David Huntington. Huntington explained the power of one of Church's most famous paintings, *The Heart of the Andes* (1859), by saying that the viewer of the painting becomes like "Adam at the dawn of human consciousness." Seeing it, one "in effect" experiences "an awakening into a higher consciousness." Above is a "cross" of "all-pervasive radiant light" that "blesses and hallows all nature." After aeons, the "mind-spirit" finally "contemplates Creation with 'Intelligence'" and as the viewer "soars" between heaven and earth in the Andes, he or she "looks out upon the world's divinity" as a "demigod."[7]

Now putatively Huntington's explication of Church reflects some elements of confessional Christianity, with references like "Adam," "the cross," "a new dispensation," "heavenly," and "reborn in Christ." But in fact, as we can see in Huntington's reading, alongside this confessional language is a very different tradition, that of Platonic mysticism, that is carried along inside the Christian tradition. Huntington's reading of the painting, using terms like "higher consciousness," "Intelligence," "world's divinity," and "demigod," is fundamentally Platonic, and I think he is absolutely right in that reading. I have long been a lover of the Hudson River School, and indeed have some of its paintings on my walls in the room where I write these words, but I did not realize fully why those beautiful, luminous paintings spoke to me with such depth and resonance until now.

The Hudson River School and the tradition of Luminist painting, as Huntington suggested, are so powerful because, although I do not think they are directly inspired by Platonism, they reflect a perspective that nonetheless is fundamentally aligned with Platonic mysticism. There are multiple aspects of this alignment. We begin with the light for which Luminism is named. While some critics have expressed doubts about the utility or need for the name "Luminism," the term captures what is truly vital about the Hudson River School and related painters of the period: in their works, light has a power unlike in any other works. Their paintings are like openings into another world, as though the beyond is somehow visible through nature's light. These magnificent paintings are transcendent immanence manifested.

What makes these glorious works so powerful—and the use of light in them is central in this—is their combination of what we might call idealism and natural realism. The paintings of Thomas Cole, Frederic Edwin Church, Asher Durand, Sanford Robinson Gifford, and Albert Bierstadt all inspire a sense of the sublime: in looking at an image of pristine nature, or of a bucolic settlement in the Catskills or along the Hudson River, one's attention is always drawn to the illumination of the landscape and to a breathtaking sense of the grandness of the natural world, of light and height and depth. Often these landscapes are in New York State, or more broadly, in North America, but others depict South American or European scenes, and they all share a sense of revelation through painting of an ideal or transcendent nature. Here, in the paintings, many of which are epic in size, is captured not only a scene of this world, but a glimpse hinting at what is beyond this world even as it is in it, of what I am terming immanent transcendence.

And there is a direct line between the Hudson River School of painting and Platonism. That link is American Transcendentalism. In *American Gurus* (2014), I devoted a chapter to demonstrating the Platonic inspiration for Ralph Waldo Emerson's philosophical essays, showing that, much more than is usually recognized, Emerson exemplified what I am terming Platonic mysticism. Emerson, in turn, was influential for the Hudson River School; moreover, he reflected a broader American understanding of how humanity in nature is not tainted by original sin but rather is able to experience the sublime there, in pristine wilderness.[8] What we see in Emerson's first work, *Nature*—his account of his own mystical experience in nature—is implicit in nearly all the paintings of the Hudson River School. Through the experience of pristine wild nature, the viewer is transported into an experience of the sublime in nature very much akin to what Emerson described as his own experience of transcendent vision in nature. The essence of this experience is the transcendence of self, which is also the essence of Platonic mysticism.

It is striking that the greatest art movements of the past few centuries, those of the Italian Renaissance and, a few centuries later, the American Renaissance, have at their center the reclaiming of Platonic mysticism in new cultural contexts. Instrumental in both cultural contexts were new translations of the great works of Platonism, in the first case, the work of Marsilio Ficino, in the second, the work of Thomas Taylor, the great English Platonist whose works then reached and inspired Emerson and others in the American Renaissance.

What we see in both Renaissances is the cultural expression of Platonic mysticism through poetry, painting, essays, and artistic and literary works that convey classical Platonism through new forms and in new contexts. This we may call contemplative art, not because it is overtly religious—it is not—but because it spontaneously manifests the contemplative experience of the artist or author and generates contemplative experience in the viewer or participant. And in both cases it is what amounts to a secular contemplative art. It has often been noted that the tradition of Platonic mysticism, in particular the *via negativa*, is not really compatible with the confessional or dogmatic traditions of Roman Catholic or Protestant Christianity.[9] It is not surprising that the American Renaissance as exemplified in contemplative art—that is, in the works of Emerson and Alcott and in the paintings of the Hudson River School—alludes in passing to Christian symbols and language, but ultimately belongs to a Platonic spirituality of nature.

Contemplative art draws us in toward the union of subject and object: by observing it, we participate in it, and that participation is also exaltation beyond our limited self. A similar experience can take place when we stand before a vast wilderness vista: we become expansive, vast, as wild and untamable as what we see. This is an inner experience, to be sure, albeit one occasioned by the setting. The word "sublime" describes what I mean here: as a verb, *sublime* means causing a substance to pass from solidity to vapor, and it also conveys an inner sense of exaltation or of purity and excellence. Contemplative art is sublime.

Contemplative science, on the other hand, is what results from engaging our faculty of inward observation to reflect upon its own nature. As B. Alan Wallace has detailed, modern externally directed science depends upon objects separate from the subject to observe and analyze. It is, particularly in its more materialistic forms, inherently dualistic. But contemplative science is not and cannot be dualistic because its subject is one's own awareness. At the same time, contemplative science does not denigrate or reject the analytical faculty of discursive reason but rather engages it to comprehend the nature of contemplative practice and experience.

With regard to the tradition of Platonic mysticism, it has some historical discontinuities, and despite the existence of various Platonic academies, as well as some committed practitioners, there is at present no contemplative Platonic tradition in the West other than what was carried along in Christianity. But contemporary authors and practitioners like Willigis Jäger do provide guidance that is broadly within the tradition of Platonic mysticism. Jäger's work in particular suggests that the future in the area of consciousness studies may be transreligious, drawing practical aspects and larger metaphysics from Buddhism, while also drawing upon the extant and venerable tradition of Platonic mysticism in the West. In the present day, East is not only East and West is not only West.

The most sophisticated model for contemplative science already exists, of course: it is found in Buddhism, with millennia of practitioners devoted to observing and clarifying the nature of the mind and vast resources. The next phase of Buddhism in the West might well be what B. Alan Wallace is proposing, contemplative observatories devoted to inner awareness and realization. From those contemplative observatories in turn may come new transreligious maps of consciousness that draw on the great wealth of the contemplative traditions of both Buddhism and Platonic mysticism, which have much in common. This is not to suggest syncretism, but rather contemplative science that draws on direct observation and verification. What in Plotinus's *Enneads* or Meister Eckhart's sermons can be empirically verified, and what would the relationship of such verification have to Buddhist teachings? That is a question for investigation, not an a priori assertion.

The prospect of such investigations, suggested by the work of Andrew Newberg, B. Alan Wallace, Basarab Nicolescu, and other contemporary authors with similar interests, is quite exciting for the future. What is required, though, is on the one hand a participatory approach to the tradition, represented in the West by Platonic mysticism, and on the other empiricism, that is, the engagement both of contemplative practice and discursive analytical reflection upon the nature and results of that practice. But that doubled approach is what we find in Plotinus's own works, which are woven out of exactly these two approaches. Plotinus is clearly drawing on his own experience, but he also is engaged in analysis of the implications of Platonic mysticism at the same time.

If contemplative art provides introductory means or entrypoints into contemplative practice, contemplative science provides analysis. And the two are not opposed, but complementary. The development of modern science and technology has required vast resources—countless laboratories, experimental grounds, telescopes, machines of every description, computers—and all of this effort, ultimately, has been devoted toward mastery of the cosmos, toward developing more and more sophisticated tools. Comparatively, almost no collective time and effort in the modern world have gone into the exploration of human consciousness and the nature of contemplative art and what contemplative science might offer us. Thus, to describe contemplative science is really a form of futurism. But it is toward such a future that this book is dedicated.

CHAPTER EIGHT

Conclusions

O ver the course of this book, we have come to see what Platonic mysticism is at its heart, exemplified in Plotinus's *Enneads*, in the *Mystical Theology* of Dionysius the Areopagite, in *The Cloud of Unknowing*, and in the many other works in this tradition. Now it is time for us to step back a bit and reflect on the significances of Platonic mysticism for the study of religion more broadly. Cognitive science, neuroscience, behaviorism, biochemistry, analytical philosophy, the social sciences, and theology have all tended toward the analysis of religion in terms of behaviors, institutions, doctrines, social structures, and biology—that is, toward the analysis of religion as an object. And without doubt light can be shed on religion and religious behavior seen through what we might call particular lenses. But at the same time, there is something at the heart of Platonic mysticism that cannot be reduced to an object, and if it is so reduced, it is de facto misunderstood.

Typically, the study of religion begins *after* Platonic metaphysics is rejected. In other words, the assumption of virtually all modern approaches to the study of religion, including those grouped above, is that Platonic mysticism is already rejected, without understanding what it is, without grappling with it, but simply asserting its being out of favor as a given. From that point, sometimes an author will look back at mysticism, but then what is discussed does not describe at all what this book has focused on.

An example of this reductionism and its unfortunate consequences is Jeppe Sinding Jensen's book *What Is Religion?* (2014), in which he writes on "The Curious Case of Mysticism as 'True' Religion." It's worthwhile to consider what he writes here because it so exemplifies the tendency we have seen to begin one's discussion of religion *after* the a priori rejection of Platonic metaphysics. Jensen seeks to divide the study of mysticism into two categories: those who hold to a sui generis model and those who hold to an ascriptive model. Those who hold to a sui generis model he thinks represent "methodological solipsism," whereas in reality, he with entirely unwarranted confidence asserts that "mystical experience has the same characteristics as other types of experience: cognitive, perceptive, conative, emotional, somatic, and so forth, but in mystical practice they are considered to be caused directly or indirectly by external forces or beings."[1] But in fact what he is asserting to be "solipsism" is just a label he ascribes to mysticism, which he clearly does not understand at all.

As we have seen, Platonic mysticism is a very specific tradition, and its center reference point, *via negativa* mysticism, is distinctive precisely because it *does not have* the "same characteristics as other types of experience." What is more, it has nothing to do with "external forces or beings." The only reason Jensen can make such assertions is that the term "mysticism" here is abstracted and removed from the broad understanding of Platonic mysticism that prevailed until the late twentieth century. Disconnected from the actual Platonic tradition, "mysticism" here becomes a floating signifier for virtually anything: all kinds of "conative, emotional, somatic" experiences of whatever type. Once one has completely disconnected from the actual textual tradition of Platonic mysticism from Plato and Plotinus and Dionysius the Areopagite through Eckhart and others, one then can make all kinds of claims completely contrary to it. That is what we see here.

Of course, Jensen is not alone in making such grand assertions about religious experience. Armin Geertz asserts that "possession and ecstasy are socialized practices," and "our biology and cognition offer no direct access to anything. Even though we think that we do, in fact, have direct access, this is an illusion created by our own brain."[2] The "ecstatic can at best be assumed to gain access to worlds constructed by the brain and society." Hence, Jensen, basing himself on Geertz's claims, calls for a "redesigned research model of mysticism" that in effect completely rejects the mystical tradition it purports to study in order to make grand claims about how it is in fact a social and cultural product without any metaphysical veridicality.

This diminution of religion to mere illusion or mental projection characterizes cognitive scientific approaches to religion more generally. Thus Pascal Boyer has developed a theory that religion is not about truth or about what is true. Rather, it is about illusion or delusion; it is a kind of self-deception whereby humans attribute agency or other "supernatural" characteristics to objects or ideas that do not in fact have them. Gods and spirits, from this perspective, are akin to a child's imaginary friends. The human mind projects supernatural beings. Boyer puts it this way: "One does learn a lot about these complex biological machines by figuring out how they manage to give airy nothing a local habitation and a name."[3]

Cognitive approaches like those of Boyer or Jensen represent a kind of inverted esoteric hermeneutics in which the exoteric faculty of rational analysis based in subject and object dualism is privileged as if it represented esoteric truth, and what is authentically esoteric, that is, based in the transcendence of subject and object, is relegated by this inversion to the realm of "illusion" or delusion. It is an interesting and unacknowledged inversion here: cognitive theory represents an attempt at a universal esoteric hermeneutic that claims to explain "how religion really works" and to provide a comprehensive model for understanding all religion. Religion results from the mind creating cognitive illusions out of natural instinctive mental processes and the esoteric key to understanding it is the power of discursive reason. But its model is based completely in dualism.

In *Minds and Gods* (2006), Todd Tremlin describes the cognitive mechanisms of agency detection device (ADD) and theory of mind mechanism (ToMM) upon which belief in "supernatural agents" and therefore religion is based.[4] Tremlin puts it this way: "Religious thought is a by-product of similar, seemingly more 'natural' forms of thinking. The cognitivist approach to religion is . . . that religious thought rests on normal mental structures and processes designed for different though functionally related purposes."[5] According to this theory, we humans evolved to be able to recognize patterns and above all other agents in our environment. Survival depended on our "agency detection" capacity in the natural world, so we are hardwired to scan for possibly dangerous agents in our environment. This capacity in turn means that we continue to scan for such agents around us, and the theory of mind mechanism means that we also seek to analyze the mental capacities of those agents. Religion derives, the theory goes, from the cognitive extension of these tendencies so that people ascribe agency and independent mental processes to projected supernatural agents.

Now what distinguishes this approach to the study of religion is that it is entirely based on subject-object dualism and on an absolute privileging of discursive reason. Other kinds of cognition paradoxically are excluded; and by the same token religion is defined as fundamentally theistic, that is, as systems of social exchange and social reinforcement built out of our natural human inclinations for agency detection and for ascription of intelligence to perceived or projected agents. Fundamentally, then, religion is defined as I/thou or as me(we)/them. Mysticism is "bypassed," to use Tremlin's euphemism, or, to put it more bluntly, ignored, because it *has* to be ignored by such a dualistic interpretive system.[6]

After the publication of *Minds and Gods*, we invited Todd Tremlin to speak at our university, and he gave a presentation on cognitive theoretical models of religion. Afterward, several students began to inquire about how Buddhism could be explained by cognitive theory, and in particular, how cognitive theories of religion addressed questions of transcendence as described in, for instance, the *Prajnaparamita Sutra*. To his credit, Tremlin responded that, ultimately, Buddhism could not be explained by contemporary cognitive theory, and indeed, represented a fundamental and unacknowledged problem for it.

Exactly the same is true of Platonic mysticism as we have described it in this book: it must be ignored if dualistic and materialistic theoretical models are to be taken seriously as comprehensive. As B. Alan Wallace observes, many experts in the cognitive sciences have "concluded beyond a shadow of a doubt that consciousness is produced solely by the brain and that it has no causal efficacy apart from the brain," despite the fact that "modern science has failed to identify the nature of consciousness."[7] He goes on to point out that materialist interpretations of the nature of consciousness might well be overturned on the basis of "contemplative evidence," but "it is a rare scientist" who would accept such data. Nonetheless, in the end, the scientific study of consciousness will, by the very nature of its subject, be compelled to take into account contemplative traditions and practices.

The truth is that, as Wallace and other scholars have pointed out, scientific theories with *a* priori materialistic and/or dualistic assumptions actually require a kind of religious leap of faith.[8] Kocku von Stuckrad goes so far as to suggest that "maybe natural scientists have taken over part of the role of the church." "Interpretations of existence are being derived from scientific discoveries," he continues, so "natural scientists are operating as the providers of meaning, and of metaphysical and religious truths."[9] But scientistic assertions of metaphysical truths on materialistic or dualistic premises are achieved by leaping over Platonic mysticism and Buddhism to get there. They *begin* with the assumption that assertions of metaphysical truth are invalid. They begin, in other words, having leapt past extensive traditions of contemplative practice and realization, motivated by faith in their materialistic premises.

This is not true, of course, of all scientific approaches. Andrew Newberg, for instance, proposed in *The Mystical Mind* (1999) a very different, much more open-ended model for understanding how science, in particular, neuroscience, and religion intersect. He and his coauthor, Eugene d'Aquili, argued that their research demonstrated at the center of the phenomenon of mysticism what they termed "absolute unitary being" (AUB). AUB corresponds pretty much exactly to what we have been describing as Platonic mysticism throughout this book. Newberg and d'Aquili describe it this way: "AUB is a state of pure awareness without the perception of discrete reality, without the sense of the passage of time, without the sense of the extension of space, and without the self-other dichotomy."[10] They continue: "[O]ur neurophysiological model of how this state is generated (i.e., by deafferentation of areas of the parietal lobe) seems to be confirmed in our brain-imaging studies of mature contemplation in Tibetan Buddhist meditators."[11] Thus, "there can be little doubt that AUB exists." It is not perceived as "subjective" or as "objective." Phenomenologically, "it seems to be anterior to either subject or object" and to be "the only state to which humans have access that eludes the categories of subjectivity and objectivity."[12] Furthermore, evidence suggests that the "pure awareness" of AUB is "nonlocal" and "unlimited."[13]

There are a number of things to point out about these observations by d'Aquili and Newberg. First, they present a scientific model that does not ignore but rather takes into account the tradition of Platonic mysticism. What is more, it does not exclude the theoretical models developed by cognitive scientists. The problem isn't with dualistic models that do, after all, present plausible models to explain aspects of human behavior and the formation of social structures. The problem comes in when those models are extended beyond their sphere and claimed to explain all aspects of human religious behavior and experience, without recognizing the history of contemplative observation that already exists in the tradition I am terming Platonic mysticism. Newberg demonstrates that a scientific model including mysticism is entirely possible.

The transdisciplinary model suggested by Basarab Nicolescu also calls for a model that integrates the sciences and the humanities, and much that Nicolescu argues in the latter half of his book *From Modernity to Cosmodernity: Science, Culture, and Spirituality* (2014) corresponds rather closely with our argument here. In particular, he observes that a transdisciplinary, integrated perspective is based on the transcendence of subject-object dualism. He argues for a "unified theory of levels of Reality," asserting that his theory of the "hidden third" "is a basic apophatic feature of unified knowledge." Nicolescu holds that we are "on the threshold of a New Renaissance," an implicitly Platonic declaration that unites the sciences and the humanities in an integrated transdisciplinarity.

The transdisciplinary model is not religious, but employs instead the word "spirituality," and indeed we might ask whether Platonic mysticism itself is intrinsically religious or not. After all, Platonism itself is often seen as belonging to the category "philosophy," not inherently to the category of religion. And one could well make the case that apophatic mysticism actually does not have to be categorized under the term "religion," which is typically defined in social, institutional, behavioral, or other similar terms anyway. It is true that Platonic mysticism is conveyed in religious traditions, notably Christian mysticism and Sufism, but mystical representatives in these traditions could be conceived as Neoplatonic passengers in a larger religious caravan to which they do not necessarily belong even if they are found there. There is much to recommend this argument.

Most important, though, is the fact that apophatic mysticism is by definition explicable as *not* being this, *not* being that, not belonging to sensory phenomena, not belonging to conceptual constructs, not explicable but only experientially verifiable. It would be logically consistent, then, for apophatic mysticism itself to be best defined as not belonging to religion. Can we say then that it is also not definable as religious? Although that would seem to be a stretch, nonetheless one is compelled to admit that this too is arguably so. Platonic mysticism points toward what cannot be described as religious, or even as experience; toward what also ultimately can't be described as absolute, unitary, or being, even if those terms have their utility.

Hence we are confronted, in this remarkable subject of Platonic mysticism, with a tradition that from its inception remains free from whatever categories and labels one might wish to apply to it. If we are today seeing the emergence of what we might term scientific religion, or alternatively, a religion of science, one could well imagine that in a thousand years, this now new religion will, whatever its other characteristics, have in it something very much akin to what we are terming Platonic mysticism. And if that is so, it is certainly because this ancient and ever young tradition well expresses truths about the fundamental nature of human consciousness that are as recognizable today or tomorrow as they were several thousand years before.

And so there is a still larger context within which we might understand Platonic mysticism, the context of the nature of reality itself. Although that context is not in vogue at the moment, in some respects it can never be entirely out of fashion. It is true that at present it may be fashionable to think about religion in externalistic and dualistic ways, and perhaps coincidentally to ignore the Platonic tradition, but nonetheless Platonic mysticism by its very nature compels us to ask whether what is referred to in the apophatic mystical tradition represented by Dionysius the Areopagite, John Scotus Eriugena, Nicholas of Cusa, Meister Eckhart, and *The Cloud of Unknowing* is pointing toward what is described in Buddhism as our own true nature, as absolute space, or as primordial consciousness.

For the largest context is our search as human beings for who and what we really are, and for the metaphysics that help make our own true nature and that of the cosmos comprehensible to us. Are we really to think that we each construct our own "truths" and that there is no ultimate truth? One can answer that question by "yes," but that is itself a religious and metaphysical claim. Against it stands the long tradition of Platonic mysticism, as well as the tradition of Buddhism. In order to truly be able to answer that kind of question, one has to first come to understand what answers have been presented by the contemplative practitioners in these enduring traditions, which present very detailed ways of comprehending our own true nature and that of the cosmos. Before we presumptuously reject them out of hand, it might first be useful to understand what they are.

Ultimately, mysticism is not just anything. It is, and has long been, understood in a Western Platonic context as a very particular tradition whose authors and practitioners explore our own human inner nature, who and what we are at heart, and what is our true nature as well as that of the cosmos. They unambiguously seek truth, and it might behoove us, as we begin to further develop contemplative science in a contemporary context, to examine and to build on what they offer us. These earlier authors and practitioners provide maps, ways of understanding and of direct comprehension that present us with great resources. We moderns have explored and continue to explore the secrets of manipulating the cosmos around us, but we are only at the beginning of the contemplative exploration of consciousness in a transreligious context. In that spirit, we conclude by pointing, not toward the past, but toward inner exploration to come.

Notes

Introduction

1. The term "essentialist fallacy" became a commonplace in scholarship in the humanities, but it is actually inaccurate, because essentialism (the view that there are essential qualities or essences that make something what it is) is a metaphysical hypothesis or assertion, not a fallacy at all. One could more accurately refer to the "constructivist fallacy" because those who assert that mysticism (for instance) is "constructed" apparently believe that a partial or limited truth (that we perceive through cultural or religious or other lenses) eclipses entirely even the possibility of metaphysical truth or transcendence.

2. These words are drawn from typical dictionary definitions of classical mysticism, for instance, from the *American Heritage Dictionary* and from *Webster's*.

3. See B. Alan Wallace, *Contemplative Science: Where Buddhism and Neuroscience Converge* (New York: Columbia University Press, 2007).

4. See Arthur Versluis, *Perennial Philosophy* (Minneapolis: New Cultures, 2015).

5. Dionysius the Areopagite, *Celestial Hierarchy*, ch. 2.

6. Dionysius the Areopagite, *Mystical Theology*, ch. 2.

7. Ibid., ch. 5.

8. See Plotinus, *Enneads*, 5.5.4. Translations drawn from Plotinus, *Enneads*, vols. 1–7, A. H. Armstrong, trs. (Cambridge, MA: Harvard University Press, 1966 1988).

9. See ibid., 5.5.3.

10. See ibid., 5.5.6.

11. See ibid., 5.5.7.

12. See ibid., 5.5.8.

13. See ibid., 5.

14. Ibid., 6.4.14.

15. Ibid., 6.5.10.
16. Ibid., 6.5.11.
17. 1. See Evelyn Underhill, *Mysticism: The Nature and Development of Man's Spiritual Consciousness* (New York: E. P. Dutton, 1911).

Chapter One

1. Walter Burkert, *Ancient Mystery Cults* (Cambridge: Harvard University Press, 1987), 18–25, especially 24, on "magic" as one of the main aspects of the Mysteries.
2. See Plato, *Phaedrus*, ~250.
3. Ibid., ~256.
4. Plato, *Symposium*, ~212.
5. Plotinus, *Enneads*, 5.6.1.
6. Ibid., 5.8.10.
7. Ibid., 5.8.12.
8. Ibid., 5.5.10.
9. Ibid., 5.5.11.
10. Ibid., 5.5.12.
11. Ibid.
12. Ibid., 5.9.1.
13. Ibid., 5.9.2.
14. Ibid., 5.9.8.
15. See Willigis Jäger, *Mysticism for Modern Times*, trans. Paul Shepherd (Liguori, MO: Liguori/Triumph, 2006), xxi–xxii.
16. Ibid., xxii.
17. See Vladimir Lossky, *The Vision of God*, trans. Ashleigh Moorhouse (London: Faith, 1963), 99–110.
18. See Nancy Hudson, "Theosis in the Greek Tradition," in *Becoming God: The Doctrine of Theosis in Nicholas of Cusa* (Washington, DC: Catholic University Press of America, 2007), 37–38.
19. See Arthur Versluis, *Theosophia: Hidden Dimensions of Christianity* (Stockbridge, MA: Lindisfarne, 1994).
20. See James McEvoy, trans., *Mystical Theology: The Glosses by Thomas Gallus and the Commentary of Robert Grosseteste on* De Mystica Theologica (Leuven: Peeters, 2003), and L. Michael Harrington, trans. *A Thirteenth-century Textbook of Mystical Theology at the University of Paris* (Leuven: Peeters, 2004).
21. See Jasper Hopkins, *Nicholas of Cusa's Dialectical Mysticism* (Minneapolis: Banning, 1985), 20–21.
22. See *De Filiatione Dei*, 2.61, cited in Hudson, *Theosis*, 157.
23. Nicholas of Cusa, *Of Learned Ignorance*, trans. G. Heron (New Haven: Yale University Press, 1954), 60–61.

24. Ibid., 173.

25. See Marguerite Porete, *Mirror of Simple Souls*, trans. Ellen Babinsky (New York: Paulist, 1993), 192.

26. See Kurt Ruh, *Geschichte der abendländischen Mystik*. 4 Bände (Munich: C. H. Beck, 1990–1999), 2.351. See also Wolfgang Riehle, *The Secret Within: Hermits, Recluses, and Spiritual Outsiders in Medieval England* (Ithaca: Cornell University Press, 2014), 136.

27. See Riehle, *The Secret Within*, 131–39.

28. Simon Tugwell, "Preface," in *The Cloud of Unknowing*, ed. James Walsh (New York: Paulist, 1981), xiv.

29. See James Walsh, ed., *The Cloud of Unknowing*, ch. 68, 252.

30. See ibid., ch. 69, 253. Walsh, in a gloss on this passage, remarks that "the author is here summarizing the directives of Denis's [Dionysius's] *Mystical Theology*, and especially the main text, which has been his concern throughout the whole book."

31. See George Panichas, "The Greek Spirit and the Mysticism of Henry More," *Greek Orthodox Theological Review* 2 (1956): 42.

32. Ibid.

33. See Robert Crocker, "Mysticism and Enthusiasm in Henry More," in *Henry More (1614–1687): Tercentenary Studies*, ed. Sarah Hutton and Robert Crocker (Dordrecht: Kluwer, 1990), 138.

34. Ibid.

35. Henry More, *An Antidote Against Atheism* (London: James Flesher, 1653), 13.

36. See Richard Ward, *The Life of the Learned and Pious Dr. Henry More* (London: Joseph Downing, 1710), 42.

37. Panichas, "The Greek Spirit," 49.

38. See Frederick Powicke, *The Cambridge Platonists* (Cambridge: Harvard University Press, 1926), 87.

39. Quoted by Powicke, 99. Powicke gives no citation, but this quotation is actually from John Smith, *Attaining to Divine Knowledge*, found for instance in E. Campagnac, ed., *The Cambridge Platonists* (Oxford: Clarendon, 1901), 96–97.

40. E. T. Campagnac, ed., 80.

41. See C. A. Patrides, *The Cambridge Platonists* (Cambridge, MA: Harvard University Press, 1970), 158.

42. Ibid., 159.

43. Ibid., 158.

44. Ralph Waldo Emerson, *Nature*, in *The Collected Works of Ralph Waldo Emerson* (Cambridge: Harvard University Press, 1971), 1.7.

45. Ibid., 1.10.

46. Ibid.

47. Ibid., 1.30.

48. Ibid., 1.38.

49. Ibid.

50. Ibid., 1.39–40.

51. Ibid., 1.43.

52. Emerson, *Essays: First Series*, 2.160–61.

53. Ibid., 2.163.

54. Ibid., 2.170.

55. Frothingham, *Transcendentalism*, 123–24.

56. Ibid., 124.

57. David Tacey, *The Darkening Spirit: Jung, Spirituality, Religion* (London: Routledge, 2013), 130.

58. Ibid., 132.

59. Ibid., 139–40.

60. The opposite of a "religionist" is presumably an "externalist," that is, someone who systematically maintains an external approach and distance from the subject and who systematically avoids any religious or metaphysical implications or meaning.

61. Mircea Eliade, *Myths, Dreams, and Mysteries* (New York: Harper, 1960), 50.

62. Ibid., 52.

63. Ibid., 53.

64. See Mircea Eliade, *Myth and Reality* (New York: Harper and Row, 1963), 137–38. See also Eliade, *Myths, Dreams, and Mysteries*, 55, in particular, that "it is historicism that definitely secularizes Time, by refusing to admit the distinction between a fabulous Time of the *beginnings*, and the time that has succeeded it." Eliade sardonically then observes that "one cannot be unmoved by this grandiose asceticism [of self-limitation to mere historicism, viewing time as a succession of ordinary events without any admission that timelessness exists] that the European mind has imposed upon itself; by this frightful humiliation, self-inflicted, as if in atonement for its innumerable sins of pride."

65. Eliade, *Myth and Reality*, 138.

66. Ibid., 139.

67. See Mircea Eliade, *Patterns in Comparative Religion* (Cleveland: Meridian, 1963), 429–30. Eliade writes, "Every myth, whatever its nature, recounts an event that took place *in illo tempore*, and constitutes as a result, a precedent and pattern for all the actions and 'situations' later to repeat that event. Every ritual, and every meaningful act that man performs, repeats a mythical archetype; and as we say, this repetition involves the abolition of profane time and the placing of man in a magico-religious time which has no connection with succession in the true sense, but forms the 'eternal now' of mythical time.'" Hence, "anyone who performs any rite transcends profane time and space." This whole passage, as so much of Eliade's work, is infused by an elegantly compressed form of Platonism.

68. H. T. Hakl, *Eranos: An Intellectual Alternative History of the Twentieth Century*, trans. C. McIntosh (Sheffield, UK: Equinox, 2013), 210.

69. Ibid., 215–17.

70. Ibid., 218.

71. See Arthur Versluis, *American Transcendentalism and Asian Religions* (New York: Oxford University Press, 1993).

72. See on Merrell-Wolff and Bernadette Roberts, Arthur Versluis, *American Gurus: From Transcendentalism to New Age Religion* (New York: Oxford University Press, 2014), 84–88, 175–78.

73. Robert E. Kennedy, *Zen Spirit, Christian Spirit: The Place of Zen in Christian Life* (New York: Bloomsbury, 1995).

74. William Johnston, *Christian Zen: A Way of Meditation* (New York: Fordham University Press, 1997).

75. See *The Willigis Jäger Foundation*, http://willigisjaeger-foundation. com/willigis-jaeger/97-portrait.html.

76. See Willigis Jäger, *Contemplation: A Christian Path* (Liguori, MO: Triumph, 1994), 32–40.

77. Willigis Jäger, *Search for the Meaning of Life: Essays and Reflections on the Mystical Experience* (Liguori, MO: Triumph, 1995), 118–30.

78. Ibid., 78.

79. See Jäger, *Mysticism for Modern Times*, 31.

80. Ibid., 36.

81. Cp. also ibid., 36, xxi.

Chapter Two

1. See Eleanor Gregory, *An Introduction to Christian Mysticism* (London: H. R. Allenson, 1901), 22.

2. See Emily Herman, *The Meaning and Value of Mysticism* (London: James Clark, 1922), vii

3. Ibid., 256; see also a comparable list on 250.

4. Ibid., 260.

5. Ibid., 261–63.

6. Ibid., 265.

7. For instance, Ernst Troeltsch, *Theologische Literaturzeitung* (1912), 727, cited in Herman, 266.

8. See Herman, *The Meaning and Value of Mysticism*, 272, citing Eduoard Récéjac, *Essay on the Bases of the Mystic Knowledge*, trans. Sara Carr Upton (New York: Scribner's 1899), 95, 98–99, a translation of *Essai sur les fondements de la connaissance mystique* (Paris: Alcan, 1896).

9. Friedrich von Hügel, *The Mystical Element of Religion As Studied in Saint Catherine of Genoa and Her Friends*, 2 vols. (London: Dent, 1923), 1.234–35.

10. Ibid., 2.91–99.

11. Eduoard Récéjac, *Essay on the Bases of the Mystic Knowledge*, trans. Sara Carr Upton (New York: Scribner's 1899), 88.

12. Ibid., 89.

13. Ibid., 90.

14. Cuthbert Butler, *Western Mysticism: The Teaching of Saints Augustine, Gregory, and Bernard on Contemplation and the Contemplative Life* (New York: E. P. Dutton, 1922/1951 ed.), lviii.

15. Ibid., 130, 232.

16. William Ralph Inge, *Mysticism in Religion* (London: Hutchinson's University Library, 1947), 10. Likewise, see in *The Religious Philosophy of Plotinus and Some Modern Philosophies of Religion* (London: Lindsey Press, 1914), 28–29, where he makes clear that Plotinus is "by far the greatest thinker" among all the philosophical mystics and that mysticism must be understood in this Platonic context. See also *The Philosophy of Plotinus*, 2 vols. (London: Longmans Green, 1918); and *Christian Mysticism* (London: Methuen, 1899).

17. See Arthur Devine, *A Manual of Mystical Theology: The Extraordinary Graces of the Supernatural Life Explained* (London: R. and T. Washbourne, 1903), 56–57.

18. Rufus Jones, *The Flowering of Mysticism* (London: Macmillan, 1939), 26, 28. For Jones's differentiation between "New Testament" and Platonic mysticism, see *Flowering*, 6.

19. Rufus Jones, *Studies in Mystical Religion* (London: Macmillan, 1909), 58.

20. Ibid., 58–79.

21. Rufus Jones, *The Flowering of Mysticism: The Friends of God in the Fourteenth Century* (New York: Macmillan, 1939/1971), 26, 28.

22. Ibid., 28.

23. Edward Ingram Watkin, *The Philosophy of Mysticism* (London: Grant Richards, 1920), 11.

24. Alfred Sharpe, *Mysticism, Its True Nature and Value* (London: Sands, 1910), 146–58.

25. Arthur Chandler, *Ara Coeli: An Essay in Mystical Theology* (London: Methuen, 1909), 122–26.

26. See Richard Maurice Bucke, *Cosmic Consciousness: A Study in the Evolution of the Human Mind* (Philadelphia: Innes and Sons, 1901), 72–74. See also *Richard Maurice Bucke, Medical Mystic: Letters of Dr. Bucke to Walt Whitman and His Friends*, ed. Artem Lozynsky (Detroit: Wayne State University Press, 1977).

27. Bucke, *Cosmic Consciousness*, 74–75.

28. Ibid., 76.

29. Ibid., 240.

30. Ibid., 253

30. William James, *Varieties of Religious Experience: A Study in Human Nature* (New York: Random House, 1902), 6.

31. Ibid., 370.

32. Ibid., 371–72.

33. Ibid., 374.

34. Ibid., 374–76.

35. Ibid., 378–79.

36. Ibid., 381–82.

37. Ibid., 407–14.

38. Ibid., 414.

39. Ibid.

40. Ibid., 419.

41. Ibid., 422, 421–47.

42. Ibid., 446–47.

43. See B. Alan Wallace, *Contemplative Science: Where Buddhism and Neuroscience Converge* (New York: Columbia University Press, 2007).

44. Evelyn Underhill, *Mysticism* (New York: Dutton, 1961 ed.), 39.

45. Ibid., 83.

46. Ibid.

47. Ibid., 71.

48. Ibid., 80.

49. Ibid., 81.

50. Ibid., 331.

51. Ibid., 332.

52. Ibid., 333.

53. Ibid., 192–93.

54. Ibid., 195–96.

55. Evelyn Underhill, *Practical Mysticism* (New York: E. P. Dutton, 1915/1943), 3.

56. Ibid., 78–79.

57. See for example *Mysticism* 424–25, where she distinguishes between the confessional "accusation" that mysticism entails "annihilation" of the personality and the mystic's "Unitive State."

58. See for example Robert K. C. Forman, ed., *The Innate Capacity: Mysticism, Psychology, and Philosophy* (New York: Oxford University Press, 1998). Forman, himself a practitioner of transcendental meditation (TM) and a student of Maharishi Mahesh Yogi, couches the entire book primarily in terms of Hinduism in his introduction. See also Steven Katz, ed., *Comparative Mysticism: An Anthology of Original Sources* (New York: Oxford University Press, 2012), in which Judaism is given pride of place.

59. Forman, *Innate Capacity*, 28.

Chapter Three

1. In his *Experience and Philosophy* (Albany: State University of New York Press, 1994), 5, Franklin Merrell-Wolff remarks coyly on having met a

"Sage," and on a setting he prefers not to name in which he, fourteen years earlier, had realized "I am Atman." One has to hypothesize a connection between Krishnamurti and Merrell-Wolff at some point, for geographic and other reasons, but I have not seen evidence of this as yet.

2. See Ron Leonard, *The Transcendental Philosophy of Franklin Merrell-Wolff* (Albany: State University of New York Press, 1999), 15–20.

3. Ibid., 19.

4. Franklin Merrell-Wolff, *Experience and Philosophy*, ix.

5. Ibid., 9.

6. Ibid., 7.

7. See Leonard, *Transcendental Philosophy*, 223.

8. Merrell-Wolff, *Experience and Philosophy*, 285–86. See also Leonard, *Transcendental Philosophy*, 224–25. The term "meontic" was coined by Nicholas Berdyaev—who was inspired by the work of Jacob Boehme and his concept of the *unground*—to express something akin to what Merrell-Wolff means.

9. Franklin Merrell-Wolff, *Experience and Philosophy: A Personal Record of Transformation and a Discussion of Transcendental Consciousness* (Albany: State University of New York Press, 1994), 252.

10. Ibid., 194.

11. Franklin Merrell-Wolff, *Transformations in Consciousness: The Metaphysics and Epistemology* (Albany: State University of New York Press, 1995), 65–66.

12. Ibid., 67–69.

13. See Aldous Huxley, *The Perennial Philosophy* (New York: Harper, 1945), 212, 214, 278.

14. See Walter Terence Stace, *Mysticism and Philosophy* (Philadelphia: Lippincott, 1960). See also Richard Maurice Bucke, *Cosmic Consciousness* (Philadelphia: Innes and Sons, 1901/1905).

15. W. T. Stace, *Mysticism and Philosophy* (Philadelphia: Lippincott, 1960), 131.

16. Ibid., 342.

17. See for instance Mircea Eliade, *Patterns in Comparative Religion* (New York: Meridian, 1963), *The Sacred and the Profane* (New York: Harcourt, Brace, 1957), and *Myth and Reality* (New York: Harper, 1963).

18. See R. C. Zaehner, *Our Savage God: The Perverse Use of Eastern Thought* (New York: Sheed and Ward, 1974), 65, 10, 64–103. See also Zaehner, *Mysticism Sacred and Profane* (Oxford: Oxford University Press, 1957).

19. Robert Ellwood, *Mysticism and Religion* (New York: Seven Bridges, 1999), 39.

20. With regard to Katz's constructivist hypothesis and his critique of many scholars of mysticism, see Steven Katz, "Language, Epistemology, and

Mysticism," in Steven Katz, ed., *Mysticism and Philosophical Analysis* (New York: Oxford University Press, 1978), 22–74.

21. Don Cupitt in his *Mysticism after Modernity* asserted, "There is no such thing as 'experience' outside of and prior to language. . . . Language goes all the way down. Language doesn't copy or convey experience; language determines or forms experience as such. . . . Writing is redemption . . . Mysticism is mystical writing: that is, it is writing and only writing that reconciles conflicting forces and turns suffering into happiness." See Don Cupitt, *Mysticism After Modernity* (London: Blackwell, 1998), 74–75. The relevant works of Steven Katz include *Mysticism and Language* (New York: Oxford University Press, 1992), *Mysticism and Philosophical Analysis* (New York: Oxford University Press, 1978), and *Mysticism and Sacred Scripture* (New York: Oxford University Press, 2000). See also John Danvers's recent study of mysticism and literature, *Agents of Uncertainty* (Amsterdam: Rodopi, 2012), 67–68, for an informed, skeptical discussion of Katz and Cupitt.

22. Steven Katz, ed., *Comparative Mysticism: An Anthology of Original Sources* (New York: Oxford University Press, 2013), 5.

23. Ibid., 5–6.

24. See Boaz Huss, "The Mystification of the Kabbalah and the Modern Construction of Jewish Mysticism," *BGU Review* (Summer 2008): 1–14, in particular, 6, where he argues "we should abandon the use of 'mysticism' as an analytical tool," acknowledging its Greek origins but making those an instrument of "colonialism," and thereby sidestepping the tradition of Platonic mysticism and its uneasy relationship with dualistic monotheism.

25. Stace, *Mysticism and Philosophy*, 342.

26. Ibid., 343.

27. Walter Terence Stace, *Man against Darkness and Other Essays* (Pittsburgh: University of Pittsburgh Press, 1967), 50.

28. Ibid.

29. See Robert K. C. Forman, *Mind, Mysticism, Consciousness* (Albany: State University of New York Press, 1999), 7–8, 129, 150.

30. See Robert Forman, *Enlightenment Ain't What It's Cracked Up to Be* (Winchester, UK: O-Books, 2011).

31. Richard Rorty, *Truth and Progress* (Cambridge: Cambridge University Press, 1998), 3.

32. Richard Rorty and Gianni Vattimo, Santiago Zabela, eds., *The Future of Religion* (New York: Columbia University Press, 2005), 30.

33. Ibid., 39.

34. Ibid., 39–41.

35. Ibid., 55–56.

36. Ibid., 75.

37. Richard Rorty, *Achieving Our Country: Leftist Thought in Twentieth-Century America* (Cambridge: Harvard University Press, 1998). In this

book, Rorty marginally distances himself from the outright Marxism of Fredric Jameson, whose term "late capitalism" reflects Marxist millenarianism, but Rorty is on roughly the same page, just a slightly different point. Along with Jameson, he assumes that "once you have seen through Plato, essentialism, and eternal truth you will naturally turn to Marx," but in Rorty's case, it is just a much squishier variant than in some of the other cases (138–39).

38. See Jeffrey Kripal, *The Serpent's Gift: Gnostic Reflections on Religion* (Chicago: University of Chicago Press, 2007), 162–80.

39. Jeffrey Kripal, *Roads of Excess, Palaces of Wisdom: Eroticism and Reflexivity in the Study of Mysticism* (Chicago: University of Chicago Press, 2001), 34.

40. See Randall Studstill, *The Unity of Mystical Traditions: The Transformation of Consciousness in Tibetan and German Mysticism* (Leiden: Brill, 2005), 176.

41. See William Wainwright, *Mysticism: A Study of Its Nature, Cognitive Value, and Moral Implications* (Madison: University of Wisconsin Press, 1981), 21.

42. See Jorge Ferrer and Jacob Sherman, *The Participatory Turn: Spirituality, Mysticism, Religious Studies* (Albany: State University of New York Press, 2008).

43. See Anthony Steinbock, *Phenomenology and Mysticism: The Verticality of Religious Experience* (Bloomington: Indiana University Press, 2015).

44. See Jonathan Shear, "On Mystical Experiences as Support for Perennial Philosophy," *Journal of the American Academy of Religion*, 62, no. 2 (1994): 319–42.

45. See Huston Smith, "Is There a Perennial Philosophy?" *Journal of the American Academy of Religion* 55, no. 3 (1987): 553–66.

46. Shear, "On Mystical Experiences," 332.

47. See also Algis Uždavinys, *Philosophy as a Rite of Rebirth* (Dilton Marsh, UK: Prometheus Trust, 2008).

48. See Wallace, *Contemplative Science*, 52, citing John Searle, *The Rediscovery of the Mind* (Cambridge: MIT Press, 1994), 97.

49. Searle, *Rediscovery*, 247.

50. Wallace, *Contemplative Science*, 52–53, 106–108.

51. Ibid., 107.

52. Ibid.

53. Ibid., 108.

54. Ibid., 151–69.

55. See Eugene D'Aquili and Andrew Newberg, *The Mystical Mind: Probing the Biology of Religious Experience* (Minneapolis: Fortress, 1999), Andrew Newberg, *Why God Won't Go Away: Brain Science and the Biology of Belief* (New York: Ballantine, 2002), and Andrew Newberg, *Principles of Neurotheology* (Burlington: Ashgate, 2010).

56. See Andrew Louth, *The Origins of the Christian Mystical Tradition* (Oxford: Clarendon, 1981), and Eric Perl, *Theophany: The Neoplatonic Philosophy of Dionysius the Areopagite* (Albany: State University of New York Press, 2007).

57. Bernard McGinn, *The Foundations of Christian Mysticism: Origins to the Fifth Century* (New York: Crossroad, 1991), 23–61, 84–130.

Chapter Four

1. See Daniel Dubuisson, *Twentieth Century Mythologies: Dumézil, Lévi-Strauss, Eliade*, (London: Equinox, 2006), 191–92.

2. Ibid., 171–288.

3. Ibid., 202.

4. Ibid., 205.

5. Daniel Dubuisson, *The Western Construction of Religion: Myths, Knowledge, and Ideology* (*L'Occidentet la religion: Mythes, science et idéologie*, 1998) (Baltimore: Johns Hopkins University Press, 2003), 175.

6. Ibid., 186.

7. Ibid., 192.

8. See Antoine Faivre, *Access to Western Esotericism* (Albany: State University of New York Press, 1994), for instance, as well as Antoine Faivre and Wouter Hanegraaff, eds., *Western Esotericism and the Science of Religion* (Louvain: Peeters, 1998).

9. See Wouter Hanegraaff, *Western Esotericism and the Academy* (Cambridge: Cambridge University Press, 2012), 296.

10. Ibid., 370.

11. Ibid.

12. Ibid., 143–44.

13. Ibid., 145.

14. One might parenthetically note here that the term "esotericist" itself is quite confused, in that it might be used to refer to esoteric practitioners, or to scholars interpreting esoteric religious practices—and one has to wonder why the word "esoterist" might not refer to practitioners. Not only the scope of the subject, but even the very term "Western esotericism" is in this contemporary usage intellectually incoherent and lexically irrational.

15. Wouter Hanegraaff, *Western Esotericism: A Guide for the Perplexed* (London: Bloomsbury, 2013), 12.

16. Ibid., 14.

17. Ibid., 11.

18. Ibid., 12.

19. Ibid., 61.

20. Ibid., 171.

21. Ibid., 12.

22. Ibid.

23. See John Walbridge, *The Wisdom of the Mystic East: Suhrawardi and Platonic Orientalism* (Albany: State University of New York Press, 2001).

24. Hanegraaff, *Esotericism in the Academy*, 15.

25. See Jeffrey Kripal, "Gnosissss—A Response to Wouter Hanegraaff," in *Religion* 38 (2008): 277–79, 278.

26. Ibid., 279.

27. Ibid.

28. E. Dimitris Kitis, "The Anti-Authoritarian Choros," *JSR: Journal for the Study of Radicalism* 9, no. 1 (2014): 3.

29. See Tamir Bar-On, "The French New Right: Neither Right, Nor Left?" *JSR: Journal for the Study of Radicalism* 8, no. 1 (2014):1–44; see also the incensed response to this article by its main subject, Alain de Benoist, "Alain de Benoist Answers Tamir Bar-On," *JSR: Journal for the Study of Radicalism* 8, no. 1 (2014): 141–68. This exchange continued in *JSR* 8, no. 2 (2014), concluding with an interview with Alain de Benoist in which he definitively rejects as biased and inaccurate the scholarship on him by Bar-On.

30. See Arthur Versluis, *The New Inquisitions: Heretic-Hunting and the Intellectual Origins of Modern Totalitarianism* (New York: Oxford University Press, 2006).

31. Hanegraaff, *Western Esotericism: A Guide for the Perplexed*, 14.

32. Peter Kingsley, presenting at the Esalen Center for Theory and Practice, 8 March 2004.

33. See Arthur Versluis, *Magic and Mysticism: An Introduction to Western Esoteric Traditions* (Lanham: Rowman Littlefield, 2007).

Chapter Five

1. Arthur Versluis, Restoring *Paradise: Western Esotericism, Literature, Art, and Consciousness* (Albany: State University of New York Press, 2004), 25.

2. Northrop Frye, *Late Notebooks, 1982–1990, The Architecture of the Spiritual World*, 2 vols., ed. Robrt Denham (Toronto: University of Toronto Press, 2000), 720.

3. See on this point Randall Studstill, *The Unity of Mystical Traditions: The Transformation of Consciousness in Tibetan and German Mysticism* (Leiden: Brill, 2005), 71–73. Studstill observes that a constructivist "epistemology is self-contradictory. The claim that all experience is mediated denies the possibility of objective truth claims." It is thus "nonsensical." It is a judgment by Steven Katz and others regarding what he considers or they consider "to be an objective state of affairs, but the claim itself denies that

such judgements are possible. If the statement 'all experience is mediated' is true, one would never be in a position to make any claim about the nature of reality at all, including 'all experience is mediated.'" Those who make such a claim indicate thereby that they "consider themselves exempt from an epistemological condition that is otherwise universal." Hence "only constructivists enjoy such a privileged perspective beyond the distorting influences of context and conditioning," something that from a constructivist perspective nonetheless "mystics themselves can never accomplish."

4. See Arthur Melzer, *Philosophy Between the Lines: The Lost History of Esoteric Writing* (Chicago: University of Chicago Press, 2014), 2.

5. See ibid., 14–16.

6. Sara Rappe, *Reading Neoplatonism: Non-Discursive Thinking in the Texts of Plotinus, Proclus, and Damascius* (Cambridge: Cambridge University Press, 2005), 234.

7. Ibid., 234–35.

8. Plotinus, *Enneads*, 6.9.3.10–13; this passage is also cited in Rappe, *Reading Neoplatonism*, 238.

9. André-Jean Festugière, *Contemplation et vie contemplative selon Platon* (Paris: 1934/1950 ed.) 5: "Quand les Pères 'pensent' leur mystique, ils platonisent. Tout n'est pas original dans l'édifice."

10. Cited in André-Jean Festugière, *Personal Religion among the Greeks* (Berkeley: University of California Press, 1954), 128.

11. Ibid.

12. Albinus, quoted in ibid.

13. Ibid., 129.

14. Dionysius the Areopagite, *The Mystical Theology*, 1.3, in Colm Lubheid, ed., *Pseudo-Dionysius: The Complete Works* (Mahwah: Paulist, 1987), 137.

15. Ibid., 141.

16. Ibid.

17. See, for a brief discussion of this, Festugière, *Personal Religion*, 130–31.

18. Eric Perl, *Theophany: The Neoplatonic Philosophy of Dionysius the Areopagite* (Albany: State University of New York Press, 2007), 13, and Dionysius the Areopagite, *The Divine Names* 1.5, 593A.

19. See Proclus, *Elements of Theology* Proposition 145; see also 121 and 131.

20. Eric Perl, *Theophany* 77.

21. Ibid.

22. Ibid., 80.

23. Ibid., 81.

24. Kevin Corrigan, *Reading Plotinus: A Practical Introduction to Neoplatonism* (West Lafayette, IN: Purdue University Press, 2005), 49.

25. Ibid., 50.

26. Plotinus, *Enneads*, 5.8.11–19.

27. Emily Herman, *The Meaning and Value of Mysticism* (London: James Clark, 1922), 277–78.

28. John Scotus Erigena, *De Divisione Naturae*, 4.8.

29. Northrop Frye, *The Anatomy of Criticism* (Princeton: Princeton University Press, 1957/2000), 134–35.

30. Ibid., 136.

31. Ibid., 137–40.

32. Northrop Frye, *Architecture of the Spiritual World*, in *Northrop Frye's Late Notebooks, 1982–1990, Collected Works of Northrop Frye* (Toronto: University of Toronto Press, 2000), 5.417.

33. Ibid., 5.395.

34. Ibid., 5.376.

35. Ibid., 5.123.

36. Ibid., 5.8.

37. Ibid., 6.715.

38. Ibid., 6.720.

39. Ibid., 6.722.

40. Northrop Frye, *The Double Vision: Language and Meaning in Religion* (Toronto: University of Toronto Press, 1991), 22–23.

41. Ibid., 40.

42. Ibid., 41.

43. Ibid., 84.

44. Kathleen Raine, *Blake and Tradition* (Princeton: Princeton University Press, 1968); see also Kathleen Raine, *Golgonooza, City of Imagination* (Great Barrington: Lindisfarne, 1991).

45. See George Mills Harper, *The Neoplatonism of William Blake* (Chapel Hill: University of North Carolina Press, 1961).

46. The works of Thomas Taylor were republished by the Prometheus Trust; see prometheustrust.co.uk for details.

47. Ithell Colquhoun, *I Saw Water* (University Park: Penn State University Press, 2014).

48. Ithell Colquhoun, *Goose of Hermogenes* (London: Peter Owen, 1961/2003), 52.

49. See William Butler Yeats, *Essays* (New York: Macmillan, 1924), 33.

50. Ibid., 53.

51. Ibid., 103.

52. Ibid., 105.

53. Ibid., 116.

54. See Arthur Versluis, *American Gurus: From Transcendentalism to New Age Religion* (New York: Oxford University Press, 2014), "Emerson and Platonism," 35–51.

55. Dionysius the Areopagite, *The Divine Names*, 597B.

56. Dionysius the Areopagite, *The Celestial Hierarchy*, 141C, D.

Chapter Six

1. See Jorge Ferrer and Jacob Sherman, "Introduction," in *The Participatory Turn: Spirituality, Mysticism, Religious Studies* (Albany: State University of New York Press, 2008), 24, citing Willi Braun, *Guide to the Study of Religion* 11, Wrathall, ed., *Religion after Metaphysics*, and Jeffrey Bloechl, ed., *Religious Experience and the End of Metaphysics* (Bloomington: Indiana University Press, 2003).

2. Ferrer and Sherman, *The Participatory Turn*, 24.

3. See Mark C. Taylor, "Deconstruction: What's the Difference?" *Soundings* 66 (1983): 397, 400, cited in Ferrer and Sherman, *The Participatory Turn*, 26.

4. See, for a clear example, Daniel Dubuisson, *The Western Construction of Religion: Myths, Knowledge, and Ideology* (*L'Occidentet la religion: Mythes, science et idéologie*, 1998) (Baltimore: Johns Hopkins University Press, 2003), cited above. But see also the literature on "postmetaphysical" beliefs, including Jürgen Habermas, *Postmetaphysical Thinking* (Cambridge, MA: MIT Press, 1994), and the privileging of discursive reason characteristic of Richard Rorty and most contemporary academic philosophy, as well as critical readings of religious studies in the line of Ivan Strenski and Russell McCutcheon. This rejection is also characteristic of the constructivist interpretation of mysticism of Steven Katz and its extreme formulation by Don Cupitt. See also, for more anti-Platonism, Gilles Deleuze *The Logic of Sense*, trans. Mark Lester and ed. Charles Stivale (New York: Columbia University Press, 1990), and *Difference and Repetition* (New York: Columbia University Press, 1995).

5. On "doxastic" practice and mysticism see William Alston, *Perceiving God: The Epistemology of Religious Experience* (Ithaca: Cornell University Press, 1991), "Literal and Nonliteral in Reports of Mystical Experience," in *Mysticism and Language*, ed. Steven T. Katz (New York and Oxford: Oxford University Press, 1992), 80–102, and *The Reliability of Sense Perception* (Ithaca: Cornell University Press, 1993). In response, see Jerome Gellman, *Experience of God and the Rationality of Theistic Belief* (Ithaca: Cornell University Press, 1997), and *Mystical Experience of God, a Philosophical Enquiry* (London: Ashgate, 2001). See also "A Problem for Alston's Doxastic Practice," *Philo* 10, no. 2 (2008): 114–24.

6. The participatory approach of Ferrer and Sherman is one such complicated and ultimately unresolved solution; another is that of Randall Studstill, in *The Unity of Mystical Traditions: The Transformation of Consciousness in Tibetan and German Mysticism* (Leiden: Brill, 2005). Neither of these approaches, while admirable in different ways, resolves basic problems that in fact are resolved by a straightforwardly Platonic metaphysics.

7. See Robert K. C. Forman, *Mind, Mysticism, Consciousness* (Albany: State University of New York Press, 1999), 7–8, 129, 150.

8. See Jeffrey Kripal, *The Serpent's Gift: Gnostic Reflections on Religion* (Chicago: University of Chicago Press, 2007), 162–80.

9. Plotinus, *Enneads*, 6.9.3.10–13.

10. See Sara Rappe, *Reading Neoplatonism: Non-discursive Thinking in the Texts of Plotinus, Proclus, and Damascius* (Cambridge: Cambridge University Press, 2000), 238.

11. Ibid., 239.

12. Ibid., 241.

13. Ibid.

14. Andrew Louth, *The Origins of the Christian Mystical Tradition* (Oxford: Oxford University Press, 1981), 12–13.

15. Ibid., 13.

16. Ibid.

17. André-Jean Festugière, *Contemplation et vie contemplative selon Platon* (Paris: 1934/1950 ed.), 191.

18. See John Scotus Eriugena, *Periphyseon* (Washington, DC: Dumbarton Oaks, 1987) [680D], 307.

19. Ibid. [681A], 308.

20. Ibid.

21. Tulku Urgyen Rinpoche, *Rainbow Painting: A Collection of Miscellaneous Aspects of Development and Completion* (Boudhanath: Rangjung Yeshe, 1995), 36.

22. See Takpo Tashi Namgyal, *Mahamudra: The Quintessence of Mind and Meditation*, trans. L. Lhalungpa (Boston: Shambhala, 1986), 187.

23. B. Alan Wallace, *Contemplative Science* (New York: Columbia University Press, 2007), 20.

24. Ibid.

25. Ibid., 113.

26. Ibid.

27. Jäger, *Mysticism for Modern Times*, 9.

28. Ibid.

29. Ibid., 15.

30. Ibid., 16.

31. Ibid., 31.

32. Ibid., 37.

33. Ibid., 48.

34. Ibid.

35. Ibid.

36. Ibid., 156–57.

37. Ibid., 157.

38. See Martin Laird, *A Sunlit Absence: Silence, Awareness, and Contemplation* (New York: Oxford University Press, 2011), 76. Plotinus is mentioned on 60 and Denys the Areopagite is mentioned on 156–57, for instance.

39. Laird, *A Sunlit Absence*, 82–83.

40. Ibid., 85.

41. Emily Herman, *The Meaning and Value of Mysticism*, 279, 282.

Chapter Seven

1. *Enneads*, 1.6.9.

2. For close Neoplatonic readings of these different artists and their works, see Liana de Girolami Cheney and John Hendrix, eds., *Neoplatonic Aesthetics: Music, Literature, and the Visual Arts* (New York: Peter Lang, 2004), and Francis Ames-Lewis and Mary Rogers, eds., *Concepts of Beauty in Renaissance Art* (Aldershot: Ashgate, 1998), in particular, and Joanne Snow-Smith, "Michelangelo's Christian Neoplatonic Aesthetic of Beauty in his Early *Oeuvre*: the *Nuditas Virtualis* Image," 147–62.

3. See Aphrodite Alexandrakis, "Plotinus, Marsilio Ficino, and Renaissance Art," in *Neoplatonic Aesthetics*, 193.

4. *Enneads*, 1.6.9.

5. Ibid.

6. See Arthur Versluis, *American Gurus: From Transcendentalism to New Age Religion* (New York: Oxford University Press, 2014).

7. See David C. Huntington, "Church and Luminism: Light for America's Elect," in *American Light: The Luminist Movement,* ed. John Wilmerding (Princeton: Princeton University Press,1980), 158. See also David C. Huntington, "Frederic Edwin Church, 1826–1900: Painter of the Adamic New World Myth," PhD dissertation, Yale University, 1960, and David C. Huntington *The Landscapes of Frederic Edwin Church: Vision of an American Era* (New York: George Braziller, 1966).

8. See Roderick Nash, *Wilderness and the American Mind* (New Haven: Yale University Press, 1967/2001), 78–82.

9. See, for instance, Frits Staal, *Exploring Mysticism: A Methodological Essay* (Berkeley: University of California Press, 1975), 62–63.

Chapter Eight

1. See Jeppe Sinding Jensen, *What Is Religion?* (Durham: Acumen, 2014), 128–29.

2. Geertz, quoted in Jensen, 130.

3. Pascal Boyer, *Religion Explained: The Evolutionary Origins of Religious Thought* (New York: Basic, 2001), 330.

4. See Todd Tremlin, *Minds and Gods: The Cognitive Foundations of Religion* (New York: Oxford University Press, 2006), 75–86.

5. Ibid., 108.

6. Ibid., 124.

7. Wallace, *Contemplative Science*, 148.

8. See ibid., 149–69. See also Kocku von Stuckrad, *The Scientification of Religion: An Historical Study of Discursive Change, 1800–2000* (Berlin and Boston: De Gruyter, 2014), as well as Kocku von Stuckrad, "Science Gradually Taking Over the Role of the Church," 12 January 2011, http://www.rug.nl/news/2011/01/opinie3_2011?lang=en.

9. Kocku von Stuckrad, "Science Gradually Taking Over the Role of the Church."

10. Andrew Newberg and Eugene d'Aquili, *The Mystical Mind: Probing the Biology of Religious Experience* (Minneapolis: Fortress, 1999), 188.

11. Ibid.

12. Ibid.

13. Ibid., 189.

14. Basarab Nicolescu, *From Modernity to Cosmodernity: Science, Culture, and Spirituality* (Albany: SUNY P, 2014), 214. See also Basarab Nicolescu, *The Hidden Third* (New York: Quantum Prose, 2016), and Basarab Nicolescu and Silviu Oravitzan, *Light Within Light* (Timisoara: Editura Universitaji de Vest, 2016).

15. Nicolescu, *From Modernity to Cosmodernity*, 215.

Bibliography

Alston, William. "Literal and Nonliteral in Reports of Mystical Experience." In *Mysticism and Language*, ed. Steven T. Katz. New York and Oxford: Oxford University Press, 1992, 80–102.

———. *Perceiving God: The Epistemology of Religious Experience.* Ithaca: Cornell University Press, 1991.

———. *The Reliability of Sense Perception.* Ithaca: Cornell University Press, 1993.

Ames-Lewis, Francis, and Mary Rogers, eds. *Concepts of Beauty in Renaissance Art.* Aldershot: Ashgate, 1998.

Austin, James H. *Zen and the Brain: Toward an Understanding of Meditation and Consciousness.* Cambridge, MA: MIT Press, 1998.

Bar-On, Tamir. "The French New Right: Neither Right, Nor Left?" *JSR: Journal for the Study of Radicalism* 8, no. 1 (2014): 1–44.

Benoist, Alain de. "Alain de Benoist Answers Tamir Bar-On." *JSR: Journal for the Study of Radicalism* 8, no. 1 (2014): 141–68.

Bloechl, Jeffrey, ed. *Religious Experience and the End of Metaphysics.* Bloomington: Indiana University Press, 2003.

Blum, Jason N. *Zen and the Unspeakable: Comparative Interpretations of Mysticism.* University Park: Penn State University Press, 2015.

Boyer, Pascal. *Religion Explained: The Evolutionary Origins of Religious Thought.* New York: Basic, 2001.

Bucke, Richard Maurice. *Cosmic Consciousness.* Philadelphia: Innes and Sons, 1901/1905.

Burkert, Walter. *Ancient Mystery Cults.* Cambridge: Harvard University Press, 1987.

Butler, Cuthbert. *Western Mysticism: The Teaching of Saints Augustine, Gregory, and Bernard on Contemplation and the Contemplative Life.* New York: E. P. Dutton, 1922/1951 ed.

Campagnac, E., ed. *The Cambridge Platonists.* Oxford: Clarendon, 1901.

Chandler, Arthur. *Ara Coeli: An Essay in Mystical Theology.* London: Methuen, 1909.

Colquhoun, Ithell. *Goose of Hermogenes.* London: Peter Owen, 1961/2003.
———. *I Saw Water.* University Park: Penn State University Press, 2014.
Corrigan, Kevin. *Reading Plotinus: A Practical Introduction to Neoplatonism.* West Lafayette, IN: Purdue University Press, 2005.
Cupitt, Don. *Mysticism After Modernity.* London: Blackwell, 1998.
d'Aquili, Eugene, and Andrew Newberg. "The Neuropsychology of Aesthetic, Spiritual, and Mystic States." *Zygon* 35 (2000): 39–51.
———. "Religious and Mystical States: A Neuropsychological Model." *Zygon* 28 (1993): 177–200.
Danvers, John. *Agents of Uncertainty.* Amsterdam: Rodopi, 2012.
de Girolami Cheney, Liana, and John Hendrix, eds. *Neoplatonic Aesthetics: Music, Literature, and the Visual Arts.* New York: Peter Lang, 2004.
Deleuze, Gilles. *Difference and Repetition.* Columbia University Press, 1995.
———. *The Logic of Sense.* Trans. and ed. Mark Lester with Charles Stivale. Columbia University Press, 1990.
Devine, Arthur. *A Manual of Mystical Theology: The Extraordinary Graces of the Supernatural Life Explained.* London: R. and T. Washbourne, 1903.
Dubuisson, Daniel. *Twentieth Century Mythologies: Dumézil, Lévi-Strauss, Eliade.* London: Equinox, 2006.
———. *The Western Construction of Religion: Myths, Knowledge, and Ideology* (*L'Occidentet la religion: Mythes, science et idéologie*, 1998). Baltimore: Johns Hopkins University Press, 2003.
Eliade, Mircea. *Myth and Reality.* New York: Harper and Row, 1963.
———. *Myths, Dreams, and Mysteries.* New York: Harper, 1960.
———. *Patterns in Comparative Religion.* New York: Meridian, 1963.
———. *The Sacred and the Profane.* New York: Harcourt, Brace, 1957.
Ellwood, Robert. *Mysticism and Religion.* New York: Seven Bridges, 1999.
Eriugena, John Scotus. *Periphyseon.* Washington, DC: Dumbarton Oaks, 1987.
Faivre, Antoine. *Access to Western Esotericism.* Albany: SUNY, 1994.
Faivre, Antoine, and Wouter Hanegraaff, eds. *Western Esotericism and the Science of Religion.* Louvain: Peeters, 1998.
Ferrer, Jorge, and Jacob Sherman. *The Participatory Turn: Spirituality, Mysticism, Religious Studies.* Albany: State University of New York Press, 2008.
Festugière, André-Jean. *Contemplation et vie contemplative selon Platon.* Paris: 1934/1950.
———. *Personal Religion among the Greeks.* Berkeley: University of California Press, 1954.
Forman, Robert K. C. *Enlightenment Ain't What It's Cracked Up to Be.* Winchester, UK: O-Books, 2011.
———. *Mind, Mysticism, Consciousness.* Albany: State University of New York Press, 1999.

Forman, Robert K. C., ed. *The Innate Capacity: Mysticism, Psychology, and Philosophy.* New York: Oxford University Press, 1998.

Franke, William. *On What Cannot Be Said, Apophatic Discourses in Philosophy, Religion, Literature, and the Arts* (Volume 1: *Classic Formulations*; Volume 2: *Modern and Contemporary Transformations*). Notre Dame: Notre Dame University Press, 2007.

Frye, Northrop. *The Anatomy of Criticism.* Princeton: Princeton University Press, 1957/2000.

———. *Architecture of the Spiritual World.* In *Northrop Frye's Late Notebooks, 1982–1990, Collected Works of Northrop Frye,* vol. 5. Toronto: University of Toronto Press, 2000.

———. *The Double Vision: Language and Meaning in Religion.* Toronto: University of Toronto Press, 1991.

Gale, Richard M. "Mysticism and Philosophy." *Journal of Philosophy* 57 (1960): 471–81.

Gellman, Jerome. *Experience of God and the Rationality of Theistic Belief.* Ithaca: Cornell University Press, 1997.

———. *Mystical Experience of God, a Philosophical Enquiry.* London: Ashgate, 2001.

Gregory, Eleanor. *An Introduction to Christian Mysticism.* London: H. R. Allenson, 1901.

Habermas, Jürgen. *Postmetaphysical Thinking.* Cambridge, MA: MIT Press, 1994.

Hakl, H. T. *Eranos: An Intellectual Alternative History of the Twentieth Century* Trans. C. McIntosh. Sheffield, UK: Equinox, 2013.

Hanegraaff, Wouter. *Western Esotericism: A Guide for the Perplexed.* London: Bloomsbury, 2013.

———. *Western Esotericism and the Academy.* Cambridge: Cambridge University Press, 2012.

Harper, George Mills. *The Neoplatonism of William Blake.* Chapel Hill: University of North Carolina Press, 1961.

Harrington, L. Michael, trans. *A Thirteenth-Century Textbook of Mystical Theology at the University of Paris.* Leuven: Peeters, 2004.

Herman, Emily. *The Meaning and Value of Mysticism.* London: James Clark, 1922.

Hick, John. *An Interpretation of Religion: Human Responses to the Transcendent.* London: Macmillan, 1989.

Hollenback, Jess Byron. *Mysticism: Experience, Response, and Empowerment.* University Park: Pennsylvania State University Press, 1996.

Hood, Ralph W. "The Common Core Thesis in the Study of Mysticism." In *Where God and Science Meet* (Volume 3: *The Psychology of Religious Experience*), ed. Patrick McNamara. Westport CN: Praeger, 2006.

Hopkins, Jasper. *Nicholas of Cusa's Dialectical Mysticism.* Minneapolis: Banning, 1985.

Hudson, Nancy. *Becoming God: The Doctrine of Theosis in Nicholas of Cusa.* Washington, DC: Catholic University Press of America, 2007.

Hügel, Friedrich von. *The Mystical Element of Religion As Studied in Saint Catherine of Genoa and Her Friends.* 2 vols. London: Dent, 1923).

Huntington, David. "Frederic Edwin Church, 1826–1900: Painter of the Adamic New World Myth," PhD dissertation, Yale University, 1960.

———. *The Landscapes of Frederic Edwin Church: Vision of an American Era.* New York: George Braziller, 1966.

Huntington, David C. "Church and Luminism: Light for America's Elect." In *American Light: The Luminist Movement,* ed. John Wilmerding. Princeton: Princeton University Press, 1980,

Huss, Boaz. "The Mystification of the Kabbalah and the Modern Construction of Jewish Mysticism." *BGU Review* (Summer 2008), 1–14.

Hutton, Sarah, and Robert Crocker, eds. *Henry More (1614–1687): Tercentenary Studies.* Dordrecht: Kluwer, 1990.

Huxley, Aldous. *The Perennial Philosophy.* New York: Harper, 1945.

Inge, William Ralph. *Christian Mysticism* (London: Methuen, 1899).

———. *Mysticism in Religion.* London: Hutchinson's University Library, 1947.

———. *The Philosophy of Plotinus.* 2 vols. London: Longmans Green, 1918.

———. *The Religious Philosophy of Plotinus and Some Modern Philosophies of Religion.* London: Lindsey, 1914.

Jäger, Willigis. *Contemplation: A Christian Path.* Liguori, MO: Triumph, 1994.

———. *Mysticism for Modern Times: Conversations with Willigis Jäger.* Ed. Christoph Quarch. Liguori, MO: Triumph, 2006.

———. *Search for the Meaning of Life: Essays and Reflections on the Mystical Experience.* Liguori: Triumph, 1995.

James, William. *Varieties of Religious Experience: A Study in Human Nature.* New York: Random House, 1902.

Jensen, Jeppe Sinding. *What Is Religion?* Durham: Acumen, 2014.

Johnston, William. *Christian Zen: A Way of Meditation.* New York: Fordham University Press, 1997.

Jones, Rufus. *The Flowering of Mysticism: The Friends of God in the Fourteenth Century.* New York: Macmillan, 1939/1971.

———. *Studies in Mystical Religion.* London: Macmillan, 1909.

Katz, Steven. "Language, Epistemology, and Mysticism." In *Mysticism and Philosophical Analysis,* ed. Steven Katz. New York: Oxford University Press, 1978, 22–74.

Katz, Steven, ed. *Comparative Mysticism: An Anthology of Original Sources.* New York: Oxford UP, 2013).

———. *Mysticism and Language.* New York: Oxford University Press, 1992.

———. *Mysticism and Philosophical Analysis.* New York: Oxford University Press, 1978.

———. *Mysticism and Sacred Scripture*. New York: Oxford University Press, 2000.

Kennedy, Robert E. *Zen Spirit, Christian Spirit: The Place of Zen in Christian Life*. London: Bloomsbury, 1995.

King, Sallie B. "Two Epistemological Models for the Interpretation of Mysticism." *Journal of the American Academy of Religion* 56 (1988): 257–79.

Kitis, E. Dimitris. "The Anti-Authoritarian Choros." *JSR: Journal for the Study of Radicalism* 9, no. 1 (2014):3.

Kripal, Jeffrey. "Gnosissss—A Response to Wouter Hanegraaff." *Religion* 38 (2008): 279.

———. *Roads of Excess, Palaces of Wisdom: Eroticism and Reflexivity in the Study of Mysticism*. Chicago: University of Chicago Press, 2001.

———. *The Serpent's Gift: Gnostic Reflections on Religion*. Chicago: University of Chicago Press, 2007.

Laird, Martin. *A Sunlit Absence: Silence, Awareness, and Contemplation*. New York: Oxford University Press, 2011.

———. *Into the Silent Land: A Guide to the Christian Practice of Contemplation*. New York: Oxford University Press, 2006.

Leonard, Ron. *The Transcendental Philosophy of Franklin Merrell-Wolff*. Albany: State University Press, 1999.

Lossky, Vladimir. *The Vision of God*. Trans. Ashleigh Moorhouse. London: Faith, 1963.

Louth, Andrew. *The Origins of the Christian Mystical Tradition*. Oxford: Oxford University Press, 1981.

Lozynsky, Artem, ed. *Richard Maurice Bucke, Medical Mystic: Letters of Dr. Bucke to Walt Whitman and His Friends*. Detroit: Wayne State University Press, 1977.

Lubheid, Colm, ed. *Pseudo-Dionysius: The Complete Works*. Mahwah: Paulist, 1987, 137.

Marshall, Paul. *Mystical Encounters with the Natural World*. New York: Oxford University Press, 2005.

McEvoy, James, trans. *Mystical Theology: The Glosses by Thomas Gallus and the Commentary of Robert Grosseteste on* De Mystica Theologica. Leuven: Peeters, 2003.

McGinn, Bernard. *The Foundations of Christian Mysticism: Origins to the Fifth Century*. New York: Crossroad, 1991.

———. *The Mystical Thought of Meister Eckhart: The Man from Whom God Hid Nothing*. New York: Crossroad, 2001.

Melzer, Arthur. *Philosophy Between the Lines: The Lost History of Esoteric Writing*. Chicago: University of Chicago Press, 2014.

Merrell-Wolff, Franklin. *Experience and Philosophy: A Personal Record of Transformation and a Discussion of Transcendental Consciousness*. Albany: State University of New York Press, 1994.

————. *Transformations in Consciousness: The Metaphysics and Epistemology.* Albany: State University of New York Press, 1995.

More, Henry. *An Antidote against Atheism.* London: James Flesher, 1653.

Namgyal, Takpo Tashi. *Mahamudra: The Quintessence of Mind and Meditation.* Trans. L. Lhalungpa. Boston: Shambhala, 1986.

Nash, Roderick. *Wilderness and the American Mind.* New Haven: Yale University Press, 1967/2001.

Newberg, Andrew. *Principles of Neurotheology.* Burlington: Ashgate, 2010.

————. *Why God Won't Go Away: Brain Science and the Biology of Belief.* New York: Ballantine, 2002.

Newberg, Andrew, and Eugene d'Aquili. *The Mystical Mind: Probing the Biology of Religious Experience.* Minneapolis: Fortress, 1999.

Nicholas of Cusa. *Of Learned Ignorance.* Trans. G. Heron. New Haven: Yale University Press, 1954.

Nicolescu, Basarab. *From Modernity to Cosmodernity: Science, Culture, and Spirituality.* Albany: SUNY P, 2014.

————. *The Hidden Third.* New York: Quantum Prose, 2016.

Nicolescu, Basarab, and Silviu Oravitzan. *Light Within Light.* Timisoara: Editura Universitaji de Vest, 2016.

Panichas, George. "The Greek Spirit and the Mysticism of Henry More." *Greek Orthodox Theological Review* 2 (1956): 41–61.

Patrides, C. A. *The Cambridge Platonists.* Cambridge, MA: Harvard University Press, 1970.

Perl, Eric. *Theophany: The Neoplatonic Philosophy of Dionysius the Areopagite.* Albany: State University of New York Press, 2007.

Pike, Nelson. *Mystic Union: An Essay in the Phenomenology of Mysticism.* Ithaca: Cornell University Press, 1992.

Porete, Marguerite. *Mirror of Simple Souls.* Trans. Ellen Babinsky. New York: Paulist, 1993.

Powicke, Frederick. *The Cambridge Platonists.* Cambridge: Harvard University Press, 1926.

Raine, Kathleen. *Blake and Tradition.* Princeton: Princeton University Press, 1968.

————. *Golgonooza, City of Imagination.* Great Barrington: Lindisfarne, 1991.

Rappe, Sara. *Reading Neoplatonism; Non-Discursive Thinking in the Texts of Plotinus, Proclus, and Damascius.* Cambridge: Cambridge University Press, 2000.

Récéjac, Eduoard. *Essay on the Bases of the Mystic Knowledge.* Trans. Sara Carr Upton. New York: Scribner's 1899.

————. *Essai sur les fondements de la connaissance mystique.* Paris: Alcan, 1896.

Riehle, Wolfgang. *The Secret Within: Hermits, Recluses, and Spiritual Outsiders in Medieval England.* Ithaca: Cornell University Press, 2014.

Rinpoche, Tulku Urgyen. *Rainbow Painting: A Collection of Miscellaneous Aspects of Development and Completion.* Boudhanath: Rangjung Yeshe, 1995.

Rorty, Richard. *Achieving Our Country: Leftist Thought in Twentieth-Century America*. Cambridge: Harvard University Press, 1998.

———. *Truth and Progress*. Cambridge: Cambridge University Press, 1998.

Rorty, Richard, Gianni Vattimo, and Santiago Zabela, eds. *The Future of Religion*. New York: Columbia University Press, 2005, 30.

Ruh, Kurt. *Geschichte der abendländischen Mystik*. 4 Bände. Munich: C. H. Beck, 1990–1999.

Searle, John. *The Rediscovery of the Mind*. Cambridge: MIT Press, 1994.

Sells, Michael A. *Mystical Languages of Unsaying*. Chicago: Chicago University Press, 1994.

Sharpe, Alfred. *Mysticism, Its True Nature and Value*. London: Sands, 1910.

Shaw, Gregory. *Theurgy and the Soul: The Neoplatonism of Iamblichus*. University Park: Penn State University Press, 1995.

Shear, Jonathan. "On Mystical Experiences as Support for Perennial Philosophy." *Journal of the American Academy of Religion* 62, vol. 2 (1994):319–42.

Smart, Ninian. "Interpretation and Mystical Experience," *Religious Studies* 1(1965): 75–87.

———. "Understanding Religious Experience." In *Mysticism and Philosophical Analysis*, ed. Steven T. Katz. London: Sheldon, 1978.

Smith, Huston. "Is There a Perennial Philosophy?" *Journal of the American Academy of Religion* 55, vol. 3 (1987):553–66.

Staal, Frits. *Exploring Mysticism: A Methodological Essay*. Berkeley: University of California Press, 1975.

Stace, Walter Terence. *Man Against Darkness and Other Essays*. Pittsburgh: University of Pittsburgh Press, 1967.

———. *Mysticism and Philosophy*. Philadelphia: Lippincott, 1960.

Stoeber, Michael. "Constructivist Epistemologies of Mysticism: A Critique and a Revision." *Religious Studies* 28 (1992): 107–16.

Stuckrad, Kocku von. *The Scientification of Religion: An Historical Study of Discursive Change, 1800–2000*. Berlin & Boston: De Gruyter, 2014.

Studstill, Randall. *The Unity of Mystical Traditions: The Transformation of Consciousness in Tibetan and German Mysticism*. Leiden: Brill, 2005.

Tacey, David. *The Darkening Spirit: Jung, Spirituality, Religion*. London: Routledge, 2013.

Taves, Ann. *Religious Experience Reconsidered, A Building-Block Approach to the Study of Religion and Other Special Things*. Princeton: Princeton University Press, 2009.

Taylor, Mark C. "Deconstruction: What's the Difference?" *Soundings* 66 (1983): 387–403.

Teresa of Avila. *The Life of Saint Teresa of Avila*. Trans. with an introduction by J. M. Cohen. New York: Penguin Books, 1957.

Tremlin, Todd. *Minds and Gods: The Cognitive Foundations of Religion*. New York: Oxford University Press, 2006.

Turner, Denys. *The Darkness of God: Negativity in Christian Mysticism*. Cambridge: Cambridge University Press, 1996.

Underhill, Evelyn. *Mysticism: A Study in the Nature and Development of Man's Spiritual Consciousness*. London: Methuen, 1945.

―――. *Practical Mysticism*. New York: E. P. Dutton, 1915/1943.

Uždavinys, Algis. *Philosophy as a Rite of Rebirth*. Dilton Marsh, UK: Prometheus Trust, 2008.

Versluis, Arthur. *American Gurus: From Transcendentalism to New Age Religion*. New York: Oxford University Press, 2014.

―――. *American Transcendentalism and Asian Religions*. New York: Oxford University Press, 1993.

―――. *Magic and Mysticism: An Introduction to Western Esoteric Traditions*. Lanham: Rowman Littlefield, 2007.

―――. *The New Inquisitions: Heretic-hunting and the Intellectual Origins of Modern Totalitarianism*. New York: Oxford University Press, 2006.

―――. *Perennial Philosophy*. Minneapolis: New Cultures, 2015.

―――. *Restoring Paradise: Western Esotericism, Literature, Art, and Consciousness*. Albany: State University of New York Press, 2004.

―――. *Theosophia: Hidden Dimensions of Christianity*. Stockbridge, MA: Lindisfarne, 1994.

―――. *Wisdom's Children: A Christian Esoteric Tradition*. Albany: SUNY Press, 1999.

Wainwright, William. *Mysticism: A Study of Its Nature, Cognitive Value, and Moral Implications*. Madison: University of Wisconsin Press, 1981.

Wallace, B. Alan. *Contemplative Science: Where Buddhism and Neuroscience Converge*. New York: Columbia University Press, 2007.

―――. *Meditations of a Buddhist Skeptic: A Manifesto for the Mind Sciences and Contemplative Practice*. New York: Columbia University Press, 2013.

Walsh, James, ed. *The Cloud of Unknowing*. New York: Paulist, 1981.

Ward, Richard. *The Life of the Learned and Pious Dr. Henry More*. London: Joseph Downing, 1710.

Watkin, Edward Ingram. *The Philosophy of Mysticism*. London: Grant Richards, 1920.

Willigis Jäger Foundation, http://willigisjaeger-foundation.com/willigis-jaeger/97-portrait.html.

Yandell, Keith *The Epistemology of Religious Experience*. New York: Cambridge University Press, 1993.

Zaehner, R. C. *Mysticism Sacred and Profane*. Oxford: Oxford University Press, 1957.

―――. *Our Savage God: The Perverse Use of Eastern Thought*. New York: Sheed and Ward, 1974.

Index